ALEX CARTER

Millionaire Negotiator

*Quickly Learn Advanced Negotiation Strategies to Help You
Win Every Deal, Overcome Obstacles, and Achieve
Unstoppable Success in Business and Life*

Contents

Introduction   1

Chapter 1: The Fundamentals of Negotiation   4

    The Importance of Negotiation Skills   4

    Understanding Negotiation Dynamics   7

    Common Myths and Misconceptions   10

Chapter 2: The Psychology Behind Negotiation   14

    Cognitive Biases in Decision Making   14

    Emotional Intelligence in Negotiation   18

    The Role of Perception and Framing   21

Chapter 3: Preparation and Research   25

    Gathering Information   25

    Setting Objectives and Priorities   28

    Analyzing the Other Party's Interests   31

Chapter 4: Building Rapport and Trust   34

    The Power of Empathy   34

    Non-Verbal Communication   38

    Establishing Credibility   41

Chapter 5: Strategies and Tactics   45

    Competitive vs. Collaborative Approaches   45

    BATNA and ZOPA   49

    The Art of Concession Making   52

Chapter 6: Overcoming Obstacles   55

    Dealing with Difficult People   55

    Managing Conflict and Tension   58

    Techniques for Breaking Deadlocks   61

Chapter 7: Real-Life Case Studies   65

Successful Negotiations in Business   65

Lessons from Failed Negotiations   69

Key Takeaways   72

Chapter 8: Cross-Cultural Negotiations   74

Cultural Differences and Their Impact   74

Strategies for Global Negotiations   78

Understanding Ethnocentrism   81

Chapter 9: The Influence of Technology   85

Online and Virtual Negotiations   85

The Role of Social Media   88

Cybersecurity Concerns   90

Chapter 10: Ethical Considerations   94

Establishing Ethical Boundaries   94

Consequences of Unethical Behavior   97

Case Studies in Ethical Dilemmas   99

Chapter 11: Negotiating in Personal Life   103

Family and Relationship Negotiations   103

Negotiating for Personal Gains   107

Conflict Resolution at Home   109

Chapter 12: Mastering the Art of Closure   112

Reaching a Win-Win Agreement   112

Formalizing the Deal   115

Post-Negotiation Strategies   118

Conclusion   121

Epilogue   124

Looking Forward   124

Empowerment Through Knowledge   124

The Journey Continues   125

A Call to Action   125

Appendix A: Appendix   126

Resources for Further Reading   126

Acknowledgments   128

Introduction

N egotiation. It's more than just a dialogue between two parties seeking mutual agreement. It's an art, a science, a dance where each step matters. Whether you're closing a multi million-dollar business deal or discussing your next career move, honing the ability to negotiate effectively can make a significant difference. This book aims to empower you with the tools and understanding necessary to become a master negotiator, transforming what may seem like routine discussions into opportunities for success and growth.

Our journey begins here, delving into the intricacies of negotiation. We'll explore the principles and tactics that underlie successful negotiating practices. For business professionals, entrepreneurs, and anyone keen on improving their life skills, this book serves as both a guide and inspiration. Negotiation is not a mystery known only to a few elite deal-makers; it's a craft anyone can master with the right knowledge and practice.

No matter your background or level of experience, understanding negotiation dynamics is pivotal. Why? Because at its core, negotiation is about understanding human behavior. It's about knowing what drives people, what they fear, and what they need. These are universal truths applicable in boardrooms, markets, or even around dinner tables.

Consider this: studies show that people who negotiate effectively across various contexts generally achieve better outcomes, not just for themselves but also for teams and organizations. Imagine the implications of mastering this skill. It doesn't just change the way you seal deals; it alters how you interact, influence, and lead. The ultimate goal is to create win-win situations where all parties walk away feeling satisfied and respected.

Thus, to negotiate well is to wield the power of change. We live in a rapidly evolving world where success hinges on the ability to adapt, to pivot strategically when circumstances demand. Your negotiation skills will provide you with the versatility to thrive in such an environment. But where do we begin?

True mastery starts with understanding the basics. Chapter 1 will cover "The Fundamentals of Negotiation," laying the groundwork by elucidating why negotiation skills matter, the dynamics that often play out, and debunking some common myths. Knowing the fundamentals gives you a solid foundation to build upon.

From there, we explore the psychology behind these interactions. What cognitive biases influence our decisions? How does emotional intelligence factor into the process? Understanding these psychological principles can offer invaluable insights into both your mindset and that of the person sitting across the table.

Preparation, one of the cornerstones of success, is another crucial aspect we'll delve into. Thorough preparation can mean the difference between triumph and a missed opportunity. Knowing how to gather relevant information, set clear objectives, and analyze the other party's interests prepares you for almost any negotiating scenario.

One cannot ignore the human element in negotiation—the importance of building rapport and trust. Establishing a connection based on empathy and credibility can lead to more meaningful and fruitful exchanges. In Chapter 4, we'll examine methods to foster these vital aspects.

Strategies and tactics are fundamental and deserve their own focus. From competitive to collaborative approaches, understanding your Best Alternative to a Negotiated Agreement (BATNA), and the Zone of Possible Agreement (ZOPA), mastering these can turn you into a versatile negotiator. And then comes the nuanced art of concession making, where knowing when to give ground can actually propel you forward.

Negotiation is seldom a smooth journey. You're bound to encounter obstacles. We'll cover how to deal with difficult people, manage conflict and tension, and employ techniques to break deadlocks. Learning to navigate these challenges will boost your confidence and competence in high-pressure situations.

But theory only gets you so far. Seeing these principles in action through real-life case studies is invaluable. Chapter 7 focuses on concrete examples of successful negotiations and the lessons gleaned from failed ones, offering key takeaways that can be applied to your own experiences.

As our world becomes increasingly interconnected, understanding cross-cultural differences in negotiation becomes imperative. Strategies for global negotiations and dealing with ethnocentrism will be thoroughly explored to equip you for the international stage.

The digital age has brought forth new mediums and methodologies in negotiation. With the advent of online and virtual negotiations, the rules are continually changing. The influence of social media and cybersecurity concerns also warrant attention, as we'll see in Chapter 9.

However, negotiation isn't just about tactics and strategies; it's also about values and ethics. Establishing ethical boundaries and understanding the consequences of unethical behavior are crucial. Case studies in ethical dilemmas will help frame this complex topic, emphasizing the importance of integrity in every negotiation.

We all negotiate in our personal lives too. From family discussions to resolving conflicts at home, mastering these skills can lead to a more balanced and fulfilling life. Exploring these everyday negotiations offers practical insights that extend beyond professional settings.

Finally, closure is an art in itself. Reaching a win-win agreement, formalizing deals, and post-negotiation strategies are the concluding steps to mastering negotiation. These final chapters will provide the closure you need to implement all that you've learned.

In essence, this book is more than just a manual of techniques; it's a roadmap to personal and professional transformation. As you turn each page, you will gain not just knowledge, but the power to change the way you engage with the world. Are you ready to start this journey towards becoming a master negotiator?

Chapter 1: The Fundamentals of Negotiation

I n the vast landscape of business, negotiation reigns supreme as a foundational skill that can alter destinies and shape futures. Understanding its fundamentals isn't just beneficial—it's essential. Imagine wielding the power to turn a simple conversation into a game-changing agreement. Negotiation starts with recognizing its importance not just in boardrooms but in everyday interactions. It's about grasping the dynamics, those subtle, often unseen mechanisms that can make or break a deal. Many walk into negotiations armed with misconceptions, believing that it's all about brinkmanship or that it's merely a tug-of-war scenario. These myths only deter success. True expertise comes from debunking these misconceptions and embracing the nuanced dance of give-and-take, understanding that each party seeks a mutual benefit. When entrenched in the fundamentals, you'll step confidently into any negotiation arena, setting the stage for transformative outcomes.

The Importance of Negotiation Skills

Imagine navigating through life's myriad complexities without the ability to negotiate effectively. Whether you're closing a critical business deal, discussing a pay raise with your boss, or deciding on a holiday destination with your family, negotiation skills are indispensable. In a world where every interaction holds the potential for conflict or cooperation, mastering the art of negotiation isn't just a luxury; it's a necessity. The ability to negotiate well is a cornerstone for success, allowing individuals to turn uncertain and potentially adversarial situations into opportunities for mutual gain.

First, let's consider the profound impact that effective negotiation skills have on your career. For business professionals, being a shrewd negotiator can be the difference between sealing a lucrative contract and watching it slip through your fingers. Negotiation is often the decisive factor in creating favorable terms that benefit not only your organization but also your professional reputation. Being known as a skilled negotiator can open doors to new opportunities and create substantial value in your career path. This ability to influence outcomes positively and steer conversations toward win-win scenarios is the hallmark of leadership and strategic thinking.

Equally important is the role of negotiation in building robust relationships. Negotiation is not just about getting what you want—it's also about understanding and valuing the perspectives of others. When you're able to empathize with the other party and genuinely consider their needs and interests, you lay the groundwork for long-term partnerships. Effective negotiation fosters mutual respect and trust, which are vital ingredients for collaboration. Strong relationships built on successful negotiations can lead to continuous growth and innovation. They allow for sustained cooperation and a greater collective capacity to solve problems and seize opportunities.

One cannot ignore the psychological benefits of mastering negotiation skills. The confidence that stems from knowing you can handle high-stakes conversations and complex dynamics is invaluable. This self-assuredness isn't just useful in professional settings but also permeates your personal life, improving how you handle conflict and engage with others. This inner confidence can significantly influence your mental well-being and overall life satisfaction.

Moreover, developing your negotiation skills can make you more adaptable and resilient. Negotiation often involves navigating through uncertainty and working toward solutions despite ambiguity and incomplete information. These situations require critical thinking, creativity, and swift decision-making—skills that are transferable to virtually every aspect of life. Adaptability and resilience are essential qualities for anyone looking to thrive in today's fast-paced, ever-changing world.

Entrepreneurs, in particular, stand to gain immensely from honing their negotiation skills. The entrepreneurial journey is rife with negotiations, from securing funding and forming strategic alliances to negotiating terms with suppliers and contractors. Each of these negotiations has a direct impact on the success and sustainability of the business. Mastery in negotiation can mean better financial deals, more favorable contract terms, and sustainable growth. It can help entrepreneurs mitigate risks and capitalize on opportunities effectively. In essence, for entrepreneurs, negotiation skills are not just important—they are critical.

Let's talk about leverage. Properly understanding and utilizing leverage is crucial in any negotiation scenario. Being well-prepared with the right information can significantly tilt the scales in your favor. A negotiator who walks into a meeting armed with knowledge about the other party's interests, market conditions, and potential alternatives is far more likely to craft a favorable outcome. This preparation not only strengthens your position but also forces you to proactively think about and address possible counterarguments and barriers. Leverage isn't just about power; it's about being comprehensively informed and strategically insightful.

Beyond the boardroom and business settings, negotiation skills are incredibly beneficial in personal relationships. Families, friendships, and even romantic relationships involve a constant balancing act of needs, desires, and compromises. Effective negotiation can resolve conflicts amicably, improve understanding, and promote a harmonious living and working environment. It enables you to advocate for your needs and concerns while also valuing and appreciating the perspectives of others. This balance is crucial for maintaining healthy, long-lasting relationships where all parties feel heard and respected.

Finally, consider the ethical dimension of negotiation. Ethical negotiators aim for outcomes that are fair and beneficial for all parties involved. Integrity and fairness in negotiation build trust and long-term goodwill. It's not just about winning the immediate deal but about cultivating a reputation for reliability and ethical behavior. This ethical approach to negotiation can significantly boost your credibility and the trust others place in you, whether in business or personal settings.

In sum, negotiation skills encompass a myriad of benefits that extend far beyond merely getting a better deal. They enhance career prospects, build and strengthen relationships, boost self-confidence, increase adaptability, and carry significant ethical weight. Investing in the development of your negotiation skills is an investment in your future success and well-being. With a strong foundation in these skills, you can navigate the complexities of modern life with greater ease and efficacy, turning challenges into opportunities for collaboration and mutual gain.

These negotiation skills you cultivate will serve as your compass, guiding you through both professional terrains and personal interactions. By prioritizing the improvement of your negotiation capabilities, you arm yourself with a toolset that is indispensable for achieving your goals and fostering meaningful connections. The journey to becoming an adept negotiator opens up a world of possibilities, ensuring that you are prepared to meet the demands of any negotiation scenario with confidence and grace.

Understanding Negotiation Dynamics

For anyone looking to master negotiation, understanding the underlying dynamics is fundamental. It's not just about walking into a room and making demands; it's about perceiving the subtleties, the unspoken cues, and the psychological currents that influence both you and the other party. Each negotiation has its distinct rhythm, flow, and energy. Recognizing and adapting to these dynamics can transform a straightforward transactional encounter into a mutually beneficial partnership.

Negotiation dynamics revolve around the ways in which parties interact and react to each other. To truly understand these interactions, start by acknowledging that negotiations are inherently fluid. They're influenced by a plethora of factors, including cultural differences, individual personalities, interests, and even the physical environment. When you understand these elements, you don't just react to what's happening; you anticipate and shape the course of the negotiation to your advantage.

A key aspect of negotiation dynamics is the concept of power. Power in negotiation isn't just about having more money or authority; it's about leverage. Having a compelling BATNA (Best Alternative to a Negotiated Agreement) can significantly shift the balance of power in your favor. If you know you've got alternatives, it changes how you approach the table. You're less anxious, more confident, and this shift is often palpable to the other party, influencing their behavior and decisions.

Another vital dynamic is timing. Strategic pauses and well-timed responses can be incredibly powerful. Silence, for example, can be a potent tool in negotiation. When used effectively, it puts pressure on the other party to fill the void, often revealing their true intentions or undisclosed priorities. Understanding the ebb and flow of conversation, and knowing when to push forward and when to pull back, can turn a challenging negotiation into a successful one.

Communication plays a pivotal role in shaping negotiation dynamics. It's not just about what you say, but how you say it. Your tone, body language, and even the words you choose can either build bridges or create barriers. Utilizing active listening shows the other party that you value their input, which can foster a collaborative atmosphere. Conversely, breaking eye contact at a critical juncture might signal uncertainty or lack of commitment. Being attuned to these signals can help you steer the negotiation in the desired direction.

Let's explore the role of empathy in negotiation dynamics. Truly understanding the other party's needs, interests, and constraints can transform the process. Empathy allows you to see beyond rigid positions and identify underlying concerns that are often the real drivers of negotiation outcomes. This knowledge can then be leveraged to propose solutions that might not be immediately apparent, but which satisfy both parties' core objectives.

Factors like emotional intelligence can't be underestimated. Being able to read the room, understand the emotional states of the other parties, and manage your own emotions are critical skills. High emotional intelligence allows you to navigate difficult moments with grace, transforming potential conflicts into opportunities for deeper connection and mutual understanding.

Another crucial dynamic is the concept of framing. How you frame your proposals, offers, and counteroffers can significantly affect their reception. Positive framing, where you highlight benefits and shared gains, is more likely to lead to a constructive dialogue. Conversely, negative framing, focusing on losses or potential drawbacks, might lead to resistance and defensiveness. Mastering the art of framing is about choosing perspectives that align with the interests and values of the other party.

Let's delve into the anatomy of trust within negotiation dynamics. Trust doesn't just spontaneously emerge; it's built through consistent, credible communication and actions. If the other party senses that you're reliable and your word is solid, they are more likely to be open and collaborative. Trust can also act as a buffer in times of conflict. Even when disagreements arise, a foundation of trust enables both parties to navigate through challenges without the negotiation derailing.

The interplay between competitive and collaborative mindsets is another critical dynamic. Understanding when to adopt a competitive stance and when to shift to a collaborative approach can be the difference between a win-lose outcome and a win-win scenario. A skilled negotiator knows that overly aggressive tactics might backfire, fostering resentment and jeopardizing long-term relationships. Conversely, excessive accommodation might lead to exploitation. Striking the right balance is key.

Perception is everything. How you perceive the other party and how they perceive you can shape the entire negotiation process. Are you seen as trustworthy, competent, and fair? Do you see the other party as reasonable or rigid? These perceptions color every interaction and influence decisions. Changing perceptions, both yours and the other party's, can redefine the negotiation landscape and open up new possibilities.

Moreover, consider the importance of preparation and research. The best negotiators are those who come to the table armed with knowledge. They understand not only their own goals and limits but also the interests, constraints, and goals of the other party. This comprehensive understanding allows them to anticipate objections, propose creative solutions, and steer the conversation in favorable directions. The more prepared you are, the more you're able to influence the dynamics to your advantage.

Finally, adaptability is a fundamental aspect of negotiation dynamics. No negotiation goes exactly as planned. There will always be unexpected twists and turns. Being able to pivot, adjust your strategy, and remain flexible in your approach is vital. Stubborn rigidity is a sure path to a deadlock. Flexibility, on the other hand, allows for the possibility of discovering innovative solutions that may not have been apparent at the outset.

Understanding negotiation dynamics is about more than just tactics and strategies; it's about mastering the art of human interaction. It's about recognizing the complexities and subtleties of interpersonal exchanges and leveraging that understanding to achieve outcomes that satisfy both your needs and those of the other party. By focusing on these dynamics, you'll not only enhance your negotiation skills but also build stronger, more productive relationships in both your professional and personal life.

Common Myths and Misconceptions

Negotiation. The word itself can conjure images of high-stakes boardroom showdowns or intense diplomatic debates. For many, negotiation feels like a mysterious art, shrouded in myths and misconceptions that distort its true nature. It is essential to demystify these misconceptions to become a skilled negotiator.

One of the most pervasive myths is the idea that good negotiators are born, not made. This myth suggests that negotiation skills are a genetic gift, reserved for a lucky few who possess natural charisma and instinct. The reality is quite different. Research and real-world experience show that negotiation is a learned skill, honed through practice, education, and conscious effort. Much like learning to play a musical instrument or mastering a new sport, anyone can become proficient in negotiation with the right training and mindset.

Another common misconception is that negotiation always involves confrontation and conflict. Many people believe that entering a negotiation means locking horns with an adversary, each party armed with demands and ready for battle. In truth, productive negotiation is often collaborative rather than combative. The best outcomes frequently arise when both parties work together to identify mutual interests and create value. By viewing negotiation as a cooperative problem-solving exercise, you can transform potentially contentious interactions into opportunities for mutual gain.

It's also widely believed that successful negotiation requires wielding absolute power. This perception is fueled by popular culture, where the most cunning and ruthless character often prevails. However, wielding power without empathy or understanding can lead to short-term victories at the cost of long-term relationships. True power in negotiation comes from preparation, knowledge, and the ability to connect with the other party. Understanding their needs, fears, and desires can provide a strategic advantage far more potent than brute force.

A particularly insidious myth is the notion that you must accept the first offer to avoid offending the other party. The fear of creating a negative impression can stifle your confidence and result in missed opportunities. In reality, the first offer is often just a starting point, a baseline for further negotiation. Seasoned negotiators know that counteroffers are not only expected but are part of the process. They provide a way to explore the range of possibilities and eventually find a mutually satisfactory solution.

Similarly, the misconception that negotiation is a zero-sum game—where one party's gain is another party's loss—flawed. This win-lose mentality can severely limit the potential for value creation. In many cases, negotiations can lead to win-win outcomes, where both sides find ways to benefit. This approach, sometimes called integrative negotiation, focuses on expanding the pie rather than fighting for a bigger slice. By looking for creative solutions and considering the broader context, you can uncover hidden opportunities for agreement.

Another myth worth debunking is that emotions have no place in negotiation. The conventional wisdom might tell you to keep a stiff upper lip and bury your feelings deep. Yet, emotional intelligence—the ability to recognize, understand, and manage our own emotions and the emotions of others—is crucial in negotiation. Emotions can be both informative and influential; they can signal underlying issues, build rapport, and even serve as strategic tools. Instead of ignoring emotions, effective negotiators harness them thoughtfully, using empathy and emotional insight to guide interactions and foster trust.

One more misconception needs addressing: the belief that negotiation ends when the deal is closed. Many think once the contracts are signed and hands are shaken, the negotiation is over. However, the most adept negotiators know that the process continues beyond the formal agreement. Post-negotiation activities—such as maintaining the relationship, managing expectations, and ensuring both parties are satisfied with the outcome—are integral to the overall success of any negotiation. This ongoing attention helps solidify trust and lays the groundwork for future agreements.

Also, there's the mistaken belief that negotiating means always having to compromise on what you want. While concessions are often part of the process, successful negotiators frequently find ways to meet their objectives without significant sacrifices. They accomplish this by being clear about their priorities, leveraging their strengths, and exploring the other party's needs and constraints. There are often multiple paths to achieving a desired outcome, and a well-prepared negotiator can navigate these to achieve favorable results.

Moreover, some people are convinced that negotiation is all about tactics and tricks, a game of outsmarting and manipulating the opponent. This view reduces negotiation to a cynical, transactional endeavor. While tactics can play a role, genuine negotiation emphasizes integrity and authenticity. Building genuine rapport, fostering trust, and seeking mutual benefit usually lead to more sustainable and satisfactory agreements. Relying solely on clever maneuvers can backfire, damaging reputations and relationships in the long run.

Lastly, many underestimate the importance of preparation in negotiation. The myth often goes: "Good negotiators can wing it." In reality, thorough preparation is the cornerstone of successful negotiation. Understanding your goals, the other party's needs, market conditions, and potential challenges equips you with the knowledge to navigate the discussion confidently. Those who appear to 'wing it' effectively often do so because they have invested considerable time and effort preparing behind the scenes.

In the end, breaking free from these myths and misconceptions can radically change how you approach negotiation. The transformation begins with acknowledging that everyone can become a skilled negotiator through learning and practice. Recognizing that negotiation is fundamentally a collaborative, not confrontational, process helps you focus on mutual gains. By debunking these fallacies, you'll lay a strong foundation for developing genuine negotiation expertise. You'll understand that negotiation is not a zero-sum game, nor a realm reserved for the naturally gifted. It's a skill, an art, and, crucially, a craft that you can master through dedication and insight.

Chapter 2: The Psychology Behind Negotiation

As we delve into the intricacies of negotiation, it's crucial to understand that our decisions are rarely as rational as we'd like to believe. Human psychology plays a significant role in shaping our approach, and the nuances of cognitive biases, emotional intelligence, and perception often dictate the outcomes more than we'd care to admit. Recognizing the biases that cloud our judgment—whether it's anchoring, confirmation bias, or overconfidence—allows us to anticipate and mitigate their effects. Equally important is emotional intelligence, which facilitates understanding and managing not just our emotions but also those of the other party, fostering a more collaborative atmosphere. Perception and framing can dramatically alter the landscape of a negotiation, as the way we present information can turn a stalemate into a successful agreement. By mastering these psychological elements, we gain a powerful toolkit that transforms mere negotiation into an art, paving the way for agreements that benefit all parties involved.

Cognitive Biases in Decision Making

Negotiation is as much a science as it is an art. A key part of this science involves understanding how the human brain works, specifically the biases that influence our decisions. Cognitive biases are systematic patterns of deviation from norm or rationality in judgment, and they can significantly impact negotiation outcomes. If you want to master the negotiation process, acknowledging these biases is not just optional—it's essential.

Consider the anchoring bias, a phenomenon where the first piece of information presented becomes a reference point and influences subsequent judgments. Imagine entering a salary negotiation. If the employer starts with a lowball offer, your counter-offer is more likely to be anchored lower than it would have been otherwise. Recognizing this, you can learn to counteract it by setting your own anchor first. Start high, if you can, and let the other party adjust around your figure.

Another pervasive bias is confirmation bias, our tendency to search for, interpret, and recall information in a way that confirms our preexisting beliefs. This can be particularly insidious in negotiations because it leads us to see what we want to see and ignore contradictory evidence. For example, if you believe the other party is inflexible, you'll likely focus on signals that reinforce that belief, overlooking indicators that they might be willing to compromise. Overcoming this entails deliberately seeking out information that challenges your assumptions.

The overconfidence bias is another cognitive trap. Believing that you know more than you do can lead to risky negotiation strategies or underestimating the other party's position. Being self-assured is beneficial, but there's a fine line between confidence and overconfidence. Maintaining an attitude of realistic humility enables you to prepare thoroughly and stay flexible in discussions.

Let's talk about availability heuristic, where people make judgments about the likelihood of an event based on how easily examples come to mind. In negotiations, if you recently read a case of a successful high-stakes negotiation, you may assume similar success is easily achievable for you. This can set unrealistic expectations and lead to disappointment. To mitigate this, ground your expectations in data and analysis rather than anecdotal evidence.

The endowment effect is another bias worth noting. This is the tendency for people to ascribe higher value to what they already own. In negotiations, this often means overvaluing your position simply because it's yours. For example, sellers may set an unrealistically high price, and buyers might do the same with their offers because of this bias. Being aware of this can help you step back and assess value more objectively, making room for compromises that lead to mutual gain.

Cognitive biases can also lead to escalation of commitment, where negotiators continue a particular course of action even when it becomes clear that it's suboptimal. This is often due to the sunk cost fallacy—valuing the cumulative investment in terms of time or resources. For instance, if you've invested a lot of time into a deal, you might push forward even if it's clear that walking away would be more beneficial. To break free from this bias, consistently assess the current and future potential of a negotiation rather than dwelling on past investments.

Let's not forget about the framing effect, where the way information is presented affects decisions and judgments. The same proposal framed as a loss can evoke a completely different response than if it were framed as a gain. For instance, "If we fail to reach an agreement, we lose the potential for a $500k profit this year" sounds more daunting than, "Reaching an agreement could secure an additional $500k profit this year". Understanding how framing works enables you to craft your propositions more effectively, putting you in a stronger negotiating position.

The hindsight bias is worth acknowledging as well. After an outcome has occurred, people often see it as having been predictable, even if it wasn't. This "knew-it-all-along" effect can foster complacency, making negotiators less likely to learn from their experiences. They might attribute successes to their skill while blaming failures on bad luck. To avoid this trap, make a habit of conducting post-negotiation reviews, focusing on what can be learned from both successes and setbacks.

Lastly, the fundamental attribution error plays a significant role in how we perceive others during negotiation. This bias leads us to attribute someone else's actions to their character while attributing our own actions to situational factors. For instance, if the other party is late to a meeting, you might think they're irresponsible. However, if you're late, you might excuse it by citing traffic. Recognizing this bias helps foster empathy and more accurately assess the other party's perspective, facilitating better communication and collaboration.

Understanding cognitive biases isn't just about identifying them; it's about actively counteracting their effects. One way to do this is by practicing metacognition—thinking about your thinking. Regularly reflect on your decisions and question the rationale behind them. Are you acting on solid evidence, or are you succumbing to a bias?

Structured preparation is your ally. Before entering negotiations, create detailed plans and scenarios. Outline potential biases and develop strategies to manage them. For example, if you're prone to overconfidence, role-play scenarios where your assumptions are challenged. If anchoring bias is a concern, prepare multiple reference points to anchor your negotiation from a position of strength.

Engage in active listening. By genuinely paying attention to what the other party is saying, you're less likely to fall into the trap of confirmation bias. Seek to understand before seeking to be understood. Ask open-ended questions and encourage the other party to share their perspective. This not only builds rapport but also provides a broader base of information, helping you see the fuller picture.

Moreover, fostering a culture of feedback can be particularly useful. Encourage your team to provide honest, constructive criticism regarding your negotiation strategies and behaviors. Sometimes, others can spot biases that you might overlook. Create an environment where such feedback is valued and used for continuous improvement.

Incorporate data and analytics into your preparation. While intuition and experience are invaluable, supplementing them with hard data can provide a more objective foundation for your decisions. Whether it's market trends, financial analysis, or historical data, grounding your strategy in facts helps to counteract biases influenced by emotions and subjective perceptions.

Finally, mindfulness practices can enhance your ability to stay present and focused, helping you recognize when biases are creeping in. Techniques such as breathing exercises, meditation, and visualization can calm the mind, allowing for clearer, more rational thinking. A composed mind is less likely to fall prey to cognitive distortions.

Mastering negotiation is a journey that involves continuous learning and adaptation. By understanding and managing cognitive biases, you equip yourself with the tools to not just engage in negotiations, but to excel in them. Remember, the best negotiators aren't just skilled in tactics and strategies; they are masters of their own minds. Embrace this knowledge, practice it diligently, and watch as your negotiation prowess reaches new heights.

Emotional Intelligence in Negotiation

Harnessing emotional intelligence (EI) in negotiation isn't just a nice-to-have skill; it's imperative for mastering the art of negotiation. Emotional intelligence transforms the negotiation battlefield into a space of mutual understanding and respect. A negotiator armed with high emotional intelligence can recognize and manage their own emotions while simultaneously influencing the emotions of their counterparts. This dual capability often makes the difference between a successful negotiation and a missed opportunity.

First, let's elucidate what we mean by emotional intelligence in the context of negotiation. Emotional intelligence comprises self-awareness, self-regulation, motivation, empathy, and social skills. Each of these components plays a pivotal role in how one navigates through the often complex and emotionally charged territory of negotiation. Awareness of one's emotions helps in maintaining control and composure, especially during high-stress or contentious moments. Imagine being able to identify when frustration is clouding your judgment, then redirecting that energy toward productive dialogue. That's the power of self-awareness.

To understand the self-regulation aspect, it helps to think of a negotiator who can control impulsive feelings and behaviors, manage their emotions in healthy ways, and bounce back from setbacks. Such a negotiator avoids rash decisions, stays calm under pressure, and fosters an environment where reasonable discussions can flourish. In stark contrast, negotiators who lack self-regulation may resort to aggression, manipulation, or emotional outbursts—actions that can derail the negotiation process entirely.

Motivation, another crucial element of EI, ties directly into the objectives you bring to the negotiation table. Intrinsic motivation, where you find deep-seated fulfillment in the process itself, often propels negotiators to prepare more thoroughly and strive for win-win outcomes. Think of it as the fuel that keeps the negotiation engine running smoothly, even when the journey is fraught with roadblocks.

Empathy, often considered the cornerstone of emotional intelligence, allows you to step into the shoes of the other party. Recognizing the emotions, needs, and concerns of your counterparty equips you to respond more aptly and foster a collaborative relationship. For instance, noticing subtle signs of anxiety or discontent can prompt you to second-guess your approach and offer reassurances, opening pathways to more flexible and creative solutions.

Social skills are the final, yet equally important, piece of the emotional intelligence puzzle. Effective communication, active listening, rapport-building, and conflict resolution—all hinge on strong social skills. A negotiator wielding these skills can deftly maneuver through the labyrinth of discussions, building alliances, and steering conversations toward beneficial outcomes.

So, how does one develop and hone emotional intelligence for negotiation? The journey involves self-reflection and mindfulness, continual practice, and sometimes even formal training or coaching. Consider starting with simple practices such as keeping a journal to track emotional responses during negotiations. Analyze what triggered specific emotions and how you responded. This practice not only enhances self-awareness but also helps in crafting strategies to manage emotions better in future scenarios.

Formal training programs can offer invaluable tools and insights for developing EI. These programs often include role-playing scenarios, feedback sessions, and interactive modules that accelerate your learning curve. Additionally, seeking mentorship from seasoned negotiators with high emotional intelligence can provide practical tips and real-world examples that ground your theoretical knowledge.

In real-world applications, the benefits of emotional intelligence in negotiation are vast and irrefutable. Successful negotiators often cite emotional intelligence as the driving force behind their achievements. For instance, consider high-stakes business deals where the parties involved manage to maintain positive relationships even after intense negotiations. This outcome is frequently a product of empathetic and emotionally intelligent actions taken during the negotiation process.

However, the road to nurturing emotional intelligence isn't without challenges. One of the primary hurdles is overcoming unconscious biases. These biases can cloud judgment and prevent you from accurately perceiving the emotions and intentions of others. For example, if you unconsciously attribute negative motives to a counterparty based solely on past experiences, you'll likely misinterpret their current actions. Overcoming such biases requires vigilant self-assessment and a willingness to challenge your own assumptions.

Another challenge lies in managing emotional spillover—where emotions from unrelated areas of life affect your negotiation demeanor. Whether it's stress from personal issues or excitement over non-related successes, unchecked emotional spillover can skew your focus and decision-making process. Techniques such as mindfulness and cognitive reappraisal can mitigate these effects, allowing you to approach negotiations with a clear and balanced mindset.

One area where emotional intelligence markedly influences negotiation is in managing and resolving conflicts. High emotional intelligence equips negotiators with the ability to de-escalate tensions and guide discussions back to productive grounds. For instance, recognizing the early signs of frustration or anger in a negotiation session can prompt immediate interventions such as taking a break or reframing the discussion topic. These actions can prevent conflicts from spiraling out of control and keep the negotiation on track.

Understanding emotional triggers and their impact on negotiation outcomes is another crucial aspect. Emotional triggers can be anything that evokes a strong emotional response, often leading to knee-jerk reactions that might not serve your long-term interests. By identifying common triggers—such as perceived disrespect or unfair demands—you can prepare strategies to manage your responses effectively. This preparatory work ensures that your emotions work as tools in your negotiation arsenal rather than obstacles.

Effective use of emotional intelligence also involves leveraging emotions as a persuasive tool. Emotions are powerful motivators for action. By appropriately expressing your own emotions, you can evoke empathy and alignment from your counterparts. For example, expressing genuine enthusiasm for a proposed solution can often have a contagious effect, boosting the overall energy and morale of the negotiation process.

Lastly, it's essential to recognize that emotional intelligence in negotiation is not a static trait but a dynamic skill that evolves with practice and experience. Every negotiation is an opportunity to refine your emotional intelligence further. Collect feedback, reflect on your performance, and make incremental improvements.

In conclusion, the incorporation of emotional intelligence in negotiation goes beyond merely an advantage—it's a transformative force. By continuously developing your emotional intelligence, you don't just react to the unfolding dynamics of negotiation; you actively shape them. This shift from passive to proactive emotional management empowers you to achieve more favorable outcomes, cultivate lasting relationships, and ultimately, become a master negotiator.

The Role of Perception and Framing

Successful negotiations often hinge not merely on the objective facts at hand but on how each party perceives those facts and frames the situation. Our minds are incredible at picking up patterns, making judgments, and filling gaps, but they can also mislead us. The way information is presented— whether it's a pay raise proposal, a cost analysis, or a project timeline—can significantly influence perceptions and the eventual outcome.

How you frame a proposal can make all the difference. Imagine you're negotiating a salary. Instead of saying, "I need a $10,000 raise," consider framing it as, "Given the market rate and the value I've brought over the past year, I'm looking for a salary adjustment to align more closely with industry standards." The latter not only sounds less demanding but also provides a rationale that can make your request seem more reasonable.

Framing isn't just about making a proposal more palatable—it's about shaping the mental model of the negotiation. Humans have cognitive biases, and understanding these can give you a leg up. For instance, the anchoring bias can come into play heavily in pricing negotiations. The first number put on the table generally sets the stage for the subsequent discussion. By setting an initial high anchor, you might influence the other party to settle closer to your desired outcome.

Another essential aspect is perception. Consider two negotiators discussing a contract. One may perceive the clause "completion by Q4" as a hard deadline, while the other might see it as flexible—a best-case scenario. Effective communicators clarify such assumptions early to ensure both parties are aligned in their understanding, thereby reducing potential friction down the line.

Framing isn't exclusive to verbal negotiations; it extends to visual contexts as well. For example, in a business presentation, the way data is presented can either highlight success or mask failure. Graphs, charts, and even colors can frame the same data in contrasting lights. A downward-trending sales graph can be alarming, but if you contextualize it by showing that it's a seasonal dip and overall annual sales are growing, the perception shifts from negative to positive.

The role of perception is also evident in the concept of loss aversion, famously explored by psychologists. People tend to prefer avoiding losses over acquiring gains. If you frame a negotiation point in terms of potential losses rather than gains, you're likely to see more engagement and urgency from the other party.

Take the example of a tech company negotiating with a supplier. Instead of saying, "Switching providers could save us $50,000 annually," frame it as, "By not switching, we stand to lose $50,000 each year." The same amount of money is at stake, but the latter phrasing taps into the psychological fear of loss, potentially driving a more favorable outcome.

The way you perceive the other party also shapes the negotiation. If you view them as adversaries, you'll approach the table defensively. But if you see them as partners working toward a mutually beneficial goal, collaboration becomes easier. This shift in perception can foster a more open and productive dialogue.

Perception also comes into play heavily in cross-cultural negotiations. Different cultures may interpret words, gestures, and even silence differently. Being aware of these nuances and adjusting your framing and perception accordingly can make or break international deals. What might be seen as a hard stance in one culture could be perceived as a straightforward business norm in another.

Negotiators skilled in the art of perception and framing don't just respond to the situation; they actively shape it. They understand that every piece of information exchanged is an opportunity to steer the conversation in a favorable direction. They know that the same fact can be framed in multiple ways, each leading to different psychological and emotional outcomes.

Consider a real estate negotiation: Instead of focusing on the house's age and the cost of repairs, a skilled negotiator might highlight the property's potential, proximity to schools, and growing neighborhood interest. This frames the property as an opportunity rather than a liability. You see the same house, but through a different lens, the narrative changes, and it becomes a more appealing prospect.

One of the most powerful tools in framing is storytelling. Humans are wired to respond to stories more than raw data. Narratives help frame situations in a relatable and memorable way. Instead of bombarding clients with statistics, weave those numbers into a story that highlights how your proposal has succeeded in similar situations.

Take, for instance, a startup founder pitching to investors. Rather than just showcasing projected revenue and growth rates, couch those figures in a compelling story about how the product is changing lives, solving real problems, and has the potential for massive scalability. This emotional framing complements the rational data, making the pitch far more persuasive.

Ultimately, the role of perception and framing in negotiation is about control. It's about controlling not just the flow of information but the very lens through which that information is viewed. This subtle art can be the difference between a failed negotiation and a thriving partnership. Knowing how to frame a situation, understanding the biases and perceptions at play, and strategically guiding the conversation are invaluable tools for any negotiator.

Perception and framing aren't static; they evolve through the course of a negotiation. Effective negotiators are keen observers, constantly reassessing the other party's reactions and adjusting their approach accordingly. They understand their own biases and work to mitigate them, ensuring clarity and focus on their strategic objectives.

Successful negotiators also use questions as a framing tool. Open-ended questions can guide the other party to see the situation from a different perspective. Questions like "How do you see this benefiting both our companies?" or "What are your top priorities in this deal?" can shift the focus from what divides you to what unites you.

In sum, the power of perception and framing cannot be underestimated. It's an intricate dance of language, psychology, and strategy. Mastering this skill enables you to shape outcomes, influence decisions, and forge stronger, more beneficial agreements. With the right approach, you can turn even the toughest negotiations into win-win scenarios.

Chapter 3: Preparation and Research

P reparation and research are your critical allies in the battlefield of negotiation. Before walking into any negotiation, you must arm yourself with knowledge about the subject matter, your objectives, and the interests of the other party. Detailed, thorough research sets the stage for informed decision-making and confident exchanges, allowing you to anticipate the opposition's strategies and craft your own responses effectively. You will find that setting clear objectives and priorities beforehand not only sharpens your focus but also keeps you grounded during the negotiation process. Furthermore, a keen analysis of the other party's interests can reveal underlying motivations and potential leverage points, making your negotiation more strategic and less reactive. Just as a seasoned chess player contemplates numerous potential moves, a master negotiator should embrace the art of forethought, using every piece of available information to sculpt a winning strategy. Remember, in negotiation, as in life, preparation is not just a step—it's the foundation.

Gathering Information

Gathering information is the bedrock of successful negotiation. Without it, you're essentially going into a conversation blind, feeling your way around and hoping for the best. Accurate and comprehensive information equips you with the knowledge to make strategic decisions, understand the other party's motivations, and ultimately, find that sweet spot where both sides feel they've won.

First, let's delve into why information is so pivotal. Understanding the landscape of your negotiation arena helps you foresee potential hurdles and opportunities. It allows you to ask informed questions, demonstrating your thorough preparation and earning you respect from the other side. By arming yourself with facts, figures, and deep insights, you develop the ability to steer the negotiation towards your desired outcome. It's really a game-changer.

Now, the question arises: where do you start? One fundamental source of valuable information is your own organization. Dive deep into internal reports, financial documents, and performance analytics. What are your company's strengths and weaknesses? What are the internal goals that influence your objectives in this negotiation? By understanding your position thoroughly, you prepare yourself to present your case compellingly and persuasively.

External sources are equally crucial. A comprehensive market analysis can offer insights into industry trends, competitive positioning, and even the economic climate that might affect negotiations. Trade publications, market research reports, and economic forecasts can provide layers of data that make you a well-rounded negotiator. Don't forget to scour public records and financial disclosures that pertain to the other party. This can often unveil surprising leverage points.

Don't underestimate the power of networking. Conversations with colleagues, mentors, and industry allies can provide insider perspectives that numbers sometimes fail to capture. These interactions may offer anecdotal evidence or inside scoops that could be pivotal. Networking can also put you in touch with past negotiators who've dealt with the same party, offering you lessons learned and tactics that either succeeded or failed.

Harnessing the power of technology can also elevate your information-gathering game. Today, we have a plethora of tools at our disposal—everything from data analytics platforms to AI-driven insights. Social media, too, can be a goldmine. Look at the other party's online presence for clues about their corporate culture, recent achievements, or even complaints. By evaluating these digital footprints, you can gauge their public persona and potentially identify soft spots or points of pride to leverage.

As crucial as it is to gather all this information, you must also know how to organize it effectively. Information overload can lead to analysis paralysis, making it essential to distill down what matters most to your specific negotiation. Highlight key insights, identify patterns, and create digestible summaries that you can refer to quickly during the negotiation.

Timing plays an integral role in gathering information. Starting your research early gives you the luxury to delve deeper and cross-verify facts. It allows you to come back with follow-up questions and refine your strategies accordingly. Waiting until the last minute not only breeds anxiety but also risks missing out on critical data that could be the difference between success and failure.

Another often overlooked but critical aspect of gathering information pertains to the human element. Emotions, biases, and perceptions play a significant role in negotiations. Conducting psychological profiling, or at least understanding the likely emotional and cognitive biases of the other party, can offer an added layer of depth. Taking time to understand their personality, negotiation style, and even their personal interests can give you valuable cues for how to approach and engage them optimally.

Sometimes, what isn't said is as important as what is. Silence, hesitation, or non-verbal cues can reveal underlying concerns or priorities. Always be observant and make notes of these subtleties. They can offer invaluable information that can guide your tactics. If you keenly observe, even the layout of their office, photographs, or awards can tell you what's important to them.

Creating a database of commonly encountered negotiation scenarios with compiled information can serve as a library for future endeavors. This could include scripts, past negotiation outcomes, and lessons learned. Having this at your fingertips means you don't start from zero every time.

While pure data and hard facts hold immense weight, qualitative aspects like culture, values, and long-term visions also offer critical insights. Understanding the corporate culture of the entity you're negotiating with can assist in framing your proposals in ways they're likely to appreciate. Companies driven by innovation, for example, might value cutting-edge solutions more than cost savings.

However, gathering information is not just a one-time event. It's an ongoing process that continues even as the negotiation progresses. Keep your ears to the ground, and adapt your strategies in real-time based on new information. The world is dynamic, and what holds true today might change tomorrow. Regularly updating your database ensures that you are always equipped with the most current and relevant information.

Lastly, never discount the importance of ethical considerations in information gathering. Respect legal and moral boundaries and ensure your methods are above board. Unethical practices may not only ruin a deal but also tarnish your reputation in the long run. Trust is pivotal in negotiations, and there's no quicker way to destroy it than through underhanded methods.

In the pursuit of becoming a master negotiator, gathering information may seem like a daunting task, but it's undoubtedly one of the most rewarding. Every piece of data you collect, every insight you uncover, and every bit of knowledge you gain builds the foundation of your negotiation power. When done right, this preparation will empower you to step into the negotiation room with confidence, agility, and a strategic edge.

Setting Objectives and Priorities

In the realm of negotiation, the first and perhaps most critical step lies in setting clear objectives and priorities. This foundational element steers the interaction, giving it direction and purpose. Knowing what you want isn't just a matter of setting goals—it's about strategically aligning those goals with both short-term and long-term gains. Imagine you're navigating a ship through tumultuous waters; your objectives and priorities are your compass, charting a course to your desired destination.

Understanding your own priorities means taking stock of what truly matters to you and your organization. What are the non-negotiables? What concessions are you willing to make? These questions might seem straightforward, but the answers often require deep reflection and robust analysis. For instance, an entrepreneur looking to secure investment needs to weigh the relative importance of funding against creative control. The clearer you are about your needs, the more effectively you can communicate and advocate for them.

When setting your objectives, try breaking them down into two categories: primary and secondary objectives. Your primary objectives are the "must-haves"—those crucial elements without which the deal isn't worth pursuing. Secondary objectives, on the other hand, are the "nice-to-haves," which can be sacrificed or adjusted as needed. This hierarchical approach ensures that you remain focused on what counts, while still allowing flexibility during the negotiation process.

It's essential to set realistic and achievable objectives. Ambition is essential, but so is pragmatism. For example, aiming for a 50% discount in a negotiation may be akin to chasing rainbows if the market standard is a 10% cut. Calibration of your objectives against industry norms and the other party's limits can circumvent unnecessary friction and potential impasses. Research here is indispensable. Know the industry standard, understand your counterpart's constraints, and set your objectives accordingly.

Prioritizing your objectives is equally critical. Not every goal carries the same weight, and understanding the relative importance of each can be a game-changer. One effective method of evaluating priorities is a cost-benefit analysis. What do you gain by achieving a particular goal versus what you lose by not achieving it? This analytical approach can offer clarity and prevent you from getting bogged down by less important issues during the negotiation.

Additionally, it's wise to prepare for possible trade-offs. Trade-offs don't always signify loss; rather, they can be strategic exchanges that bring you closer to your main objective. If you're a business professional aiming to close a contract, you might be willing to accept stricter delivery timelines in exchange for a larger order. Such willingness can break deadlocks and turn a rigid negotiation into a fluid, constructive dialogue.

However, objectives and priorities aren't static; they may evolve as the negotiation progresses. Flexibility is your ally here. A rigid approach can make negotiations like a closed-loop system, while fluidity opens up new avenues and opportunities. Remain adaptable, updating your objectives based on new information or changes in circumstances. This adaptive approach lets you navigate the negotiation dynamics more effectively, ensuring that you stay aligned with your ultimate goals.

Notably, objectives should also be aligned with your long-term vision. While short-term gains are tempting, they should not be pursued at the expense of long-term goals. For instance, an impulsive decision to undercut prices drastically might win you a deal today but could wear down your brand value over time. Aligning your immediate objectives with a broader vision ensures that your negotiation efforts contribute to sustainable success.

A narrative approach to objective-setting can also be incredibly effective. Storytelling isn't just for kids; it's a powerful tool in business as well. Frame your objectives within the context of a story—how achieving these objectives will impact your organization, your team, and perhaps even the broader industry or community. This method not only helps you visualize your goals but can also make them more compelling when articulated to others.

Preparing comprehensively for negotiations also demands a thorough understanding of both parties' objectives. Utilizing open-ended questions can offer deep insights into what the other side values most. Once you understand their priorities, you can tailor your approach to create value for both sides. For example, if time is a critical factor for the other party, you might gain significant leverage by offering a quicker turnaround time. Thus, mutual understanding can lead to a solution where both parties feel like they've won.

Moreover, effective negotiation is often about finding common ground. Common objectives create a sense of partnership and shared purpose, which can smoothen the negotiation path. Envision this as a Venn diagram, where overlapping circles represent shared goals and interests. Identifying these areas can foster a collaborative rather than adversarial mindset, shifting the negotiation from a zero-sum game to a win-win scenario.

So, as you embark on any negotiation, take the time to set your objectives and priorities with precision and clarity. Know what you want, be clear on what you're willing to trade, and align your goals with your long-term vision. Remember, a well-prepared negotiator is not just someone who knows their objectives, but one who prioritizes them thoughtfully and flexibly, ready to adapt as the negotiation unfolds.

In summary, setting objectives and priorities isn't just about listing your wants and needs—it's about fostering a strategic framework for achieving them. This preparation not only equips you with the right tools but also empowers you with the confidence and clarity necessary for successful negotiation outcomes. As you advance through the subsequent chapters, you'll discover how this foundational understanding interweaves with every other facet of negotiation, creating a comprehensive roadmap to mastering the art of negotiation.

Analyzing the Other Party's Interests

In any successful negotiation, understanding the interests of the other party is paramount. It's not just about what they say they want, but the underlying needs and desires that drive those wants. Just like an iceberg, the surface-level demands often hide deeper motivations beneath the waterline. To become a master negotiator, you've got to dive below the surface and explore these underlying interests.

Grasping the other party's interests allows you to craft strategies tailored to addressing their core needs. Take a moment to think about this: you're not merely haggling over terms, you're uncovering what truly matters to them. Maybe it's efficiency, security, prestige, or peace of mind. Unveil these drivers and you'll not only find common ground but also create solutions that can turn hesitancy into willingness.

Start by actively listening. This means more than just hearing words; it's about picking up on subtleties, noticing what isn't said, and interpreting non-verbal cues. Imagine yourself in their shoes, facing their pressures and challenges. This empathy will enable you to tune into their real concerns and priorities. Through keen observation and thoughtful questions, you can gather valuable insights into their point of view.

To dig deeper, ask open-ended questions that encourage the other party to elaborate on their needs and goals. For example, questions like "What are your main concerns with this proposal?" or "What would it take for this solution to work for you?" open up a dialogue and reveal important details. These questions don't corner them into yes or no responses but invite them to share more about their motivations and constraints.

Be mindful of cognitive biases that may cloud your judgment or theirs. Confirmation bias could cause you to interpret their statements in a way that fits your existing beliefs, while anchoring bias might make the first piece of information too influential. Awareness of these biases helps you remain objective and minimizes misinterpretations.

Recognize that the other party's interests may be multifaceted. People rarely operate with a single goal in mind. There could be financial, emotional, political, or social drivers at play. For instance, a business might prioritize profit but also care deeply about corporate social responsibility. Being attuned to these nuances gives you a broader understanding of their negotiating stance.

At times, interests could be conflicting even within the same organization. Different stakeholders have different priorities, and navigating this internal landscape can be complex. The key is to align your proposals in a way that satisfies the primary decision-makers while also addressing the concerns of other stakeholders. Building coalitions within the opposing party can turn the tide in your favor.

Observation and intuition are not enough; documentation and verification can be equally critical. Validate your assumptions through data whenever possible. Market reports, performance metrics, or stakeholder interviews can provide a factual basis to support your understanding. Don't overlook the wealth of information available through public records, news articles, and industry analyses.

Balance your research with a genuine curiosity and openness to new information. Negotiations are dynamic, and being flexible in your approach is crucial. Preconceived notions can hinder your ability to adapt to new information that emerges during discussions. A flexible mindset enables you to recalibrate your strategies, making you more resilient and responsive to the flow of negotiation.

Transparency has its virtues but be strategic about the information you share. Revealing that you've done your homework on their needs can indicate your commitment and thoroughness but also restrain how much they disclose. It's a delicate balance: share just enough to build trust and credibility while holding back to encourage more openness from them.

Effective negotiators harness the power of mirroring. Reflecting back some of the other party's words and phrases creates rapport and encourages more disclosure. Phrases like "If I understand you correctly, you're looking for..." reinforce that you're engaged and invested in understanding their perspective. This technique not only deepens understanding but also fosters a collaborative atmosphere.

The context in which the other party operates offers vital clues. Industry trends, economic conditions, and competitive pressures can all influence their priorities. A supplier negotiating during an economic downturn, for example, might prioritize long-term stability over short-term gains. Tailoring your approach to these contextual factors can make your proposals more appealing and realistic.

Finally, compile all your findings into a coherent framework. This isn't just a one-time activity but a living document that evolves with new information. Regularly revisiting and updating this framework ensures your strategies remain aligned with the other party's changing interests and external conditions. Keep your insights organized, accessible, and ready for quick reference during negotiations.

Armed with a thorough understanding of the other party's interests, you'll be well-prepared to steer negotiations toward mutually beneficial outcomes. Remember, the goal isn't to "win" but to find an intersection where both parties can achieve their most critical objectives. By focusing on interests over positions, you create a fertile ground for innovative solutions and lasting agreements.

Chapter 4: Building Rapport and Trust

Often, the key to successful negotiations isn't just what you know, but who you're able to connect with on a human level. Without trust and rapport, even the most well-constructed arguments can fall flat. Building these foundational elements is akin to laying the groundwork for a sturdy bridge; it requires genuine empathy, astute observation of non-verbal cues, and the consistent demonstration of reliability. A sincere investment in understanding the other party's perspective can transform potential adversaries into collaborative partners, opening the door to mutually beneficial outcomes. When you show you're authentically engaged, not only do you make the counterpart more comfortable, but you also pave the way for transparency and honesty—cornerstones of effective negotiation. As we delve deeper into the mechanics of rapport and trust, remember that these elements aren't mere tactics but integral threads in the fabric of any lasting agreement.

The Power of Empathy

Empathy is often miscast as a "soft" skill, a nice-to-have but not essential tool in the arsenal of a business professional. This couldn't be further from the truth. In the world of high-stakes negotiation, empathy is not just a virtue; it is a powerful weapon. It enables us to truly understand the motivations, fears, and desires of the other party, laying the groundwork for genuine rapport and trust.

Empathy is not merely about feeling another's pain. It's about comprehending their perspective and using that understanding to influence the negotiation process constructively. Imagine stepping into another person's shoes and seeing the world through their eyes. By doing this, you can glean invaluable insights into what they really want and need.

Consider a seasoned salesperson negotiating a big contract with a new client. The salesperson knows that achieving this deal isn't just about pushing their product; it's about identifying and addressing the client's unspoken concerns. By empathizing with the client's pressure points and challenges, they can tailor their pitch to resonate deeply. When the client feels understood, the conversation shifts from mere transaction to collaboration.

One might wonder, is empathy innate or can it be cultivated? The good news is, empathy can be developed through deliberate practice. Start by enhancing your active listening skills. Active listening involves fully concentrating on the speaker, understanding their message, responding thoughtfully, and remembering key points. Instead of thinking about your next argument or how to counter their statements, focus fully on what they are saying. It's a subtle yet powerful shift.

Beyond listening, ask open-ended questions. These are queries that cannot be answered with a simple "yes" or "no." For example, instead of asking, "Do you like this proposal?" you could ask, "What aspects of this proposal do you feel strongly about?" Such questions encourage a deeper conversation and demonstrate that you genuinely care about the other party's views.

It's important to acknowledge that empathy is not synonymous with agreement. You can understand and empathize with someone's position without conceding to their demands. Being empathetic means you recognize their feelings and viewpoints, which can help soften their stance and make them more open to your proposals.

The benefits of empathy in negotiation extend beyond the immediate deal. When people feel understood and valued, they are more likely to engage in future transactions and partnerships. This strengthens long-term relationships, fostering a sense of loyalty and mutual respect that can be invaluable in business.

Let's not forget that we are all human, wired to seek connection and understanding. In the sterile environment of boardrooms or across a negotiating table, empathy brings a touch of humanity, facilitating conversations that are more honest and productive. The next time you find yourself preparing for a negotiation, take a moment to consider the human element. It's not always about what's on paper; it's about what's in the hearts and minds of those involved.

Empathy allows negotiators to anticipate objections and plan their responses. By predicting potential roadblocks and addressing them proactively, you can navigate more smoothly toward a mutually beneficial agreement. When the other party sees that you have anticipated their needs and concerns, they'll be more inclined to trust you and less likely to hold back in sharing essential information.

In heated negotiations, emotions can run high. Instead of reciprocating with aggression or defensiveness, employing empathy can help de-escalate tension. A simple acknowledgment of the other party's frustration or disappointment can work wonders in calming the storm. Phrases like "I can see why you might feel that way" or "I understand where you're coming from" can be disarming and pave the way for a more rational discussion.

While empathy is crucial, it should be balanced with a clear understanding of your own goals and limits. The art of negotiation lies in striking this balance— developing the emotional intelligence to empathize while never losing sight of your objectives. This balance ensures that while you are supportive and understanding, you remain firm and resolute in your pursuits.

To further refine your empathetic skills, consider role-playing exercises with a colleague or mentor. Simulating negotiation scenarios where you take on different roles can provide critical insights into how others might perceive and react to your approach. This practice helps you fine-tune your strategies and develop a more nuanced understanding of diverse perspectives.

Emotion also significantly impacts decision-making. Recognizing and respecting this emotional landscape can influence the outcome of negotiations. When people feel their emotions are acknowledged, they become more receptive to logical arguments. It's a dual-track approach—catering to both emotional and rational hurdles—that often leads to successful negotiations.

Empathy doesn't end with the final handshake. Following up post-negotiation with a thank-you note or a brief call can reinforce the connection and leave a lasting positive impression. These small gestures go a long way in solidifying the relationship and paving the way for future collaborations.

Believe it or not, showing empathy can even give you an edge over more aggressive negotiation styles. While traditional hardball tactics may yield short-term gains, they often leave lasting wounds and mistrust. On the other hand, an empathetic approach, one that seeks to understand before being understood, builds bridges and opens doors that might otherwise remain closed.

It's also worth noting that empathy encourages transparency. When the other party feels safe and understood, they are more likely to share crucial information, which can be invaluable in structuring a deal that works for both sides. Knowledge is power in negotiation, and empathy unlocks this power by fostering open dialogue and reducing defensive posturing.

Empathy in negotiation is not a zero-sum game. It isn't about losing ground to make the other party feel better. Instead, it's about creating a scenario where both parties feel they are walking away with something of value. This is the essence of win-win negotiations. By putting yourself in the other party's shoes, you can identify areas of compromise and craft solutions that satisfy both sides.

Lastly, think about your own experiences when you felt genuinely understood and valued. How did it impact your feelings towards the person who made you feel that way? Chances are, it built trust and goodwill. Now, translate that understanding into your negotiations. Use empathy as a strategic tool to build rapport, create trust, and ultimately become a more successful negotiator.

In summing up, empathy is the cornerstone upon which robust and lasting business relationships are built. It allows you to radiate sincerity, break through barriers, and establish a foundation of trust upon which mutually rewarding deals are constructed. By cultivating empathy, you not only enhance your negotiation skills but also set yourself apart in the competitive world of business.

Non-Verbal Communication

When it comes to building rapport and trust in negotiations, non-verbal communication often speaks louder than words. This form of communication encompasses everything from body language and facial expressions to eye contact and even the tone of your voice. Understanding and mastering non-verbal cues is crucial for any business professional or entrepreneur looking to gain an edge in negotiations.

It's often said that over 90% of communication is non-verbal. While the exact percentage can be debated, the importance of non-verbal signals can't be overstated. They can affirm or contradict your spoken words, revealing your true feelings and intentions. A simple smile, a handshake, or even the tilt of your head can make a world of difference when you're trying to build trust. People tend to believe what they see more than what they hear. If your body language aligns with your words, it enhances your credibility and fosters trust. Conversely, mixed messages can quickly erode any sense of reliability you've worked to establish.

One of the first aspects of non-verbal communication to master is eye contact. It's a powerful tool that can convey confidence and sincerity. Maintaining steady eye contact demonstrates that you are engaged and interested in the conversation. Be careful not to overdo it, as too much eye contact can come off as aggressive or confrontational. Instead, aim for a balanced approach—enough to show that you're invested, but not so much that it makes the other person uncomfortable.

Equally important is your posture. The way you sit or stand can speak volumes about your attitude and state of mind. Sitting up straight with your shoulders back projects confidence and attentiveness, while slouching might give the impression of disinterest or insecurity. Open body language, such as uncrossed arms and leaning slightly forward, invites a more open and engaging conversation. It signals to the other party that you are receptive, cooperative, and eager to listen. Subtle cues like nodding can also show that you're paying attention and agree with what's being said.

Facial expressions are another critical element. Smiling, for instance, can instantly create a friendly and welcoming atmosphere. A genuine smile reaches the eyes and can make the other party feel valued and understood. On the other hand, frowning or showing signs of impatience can quickly derail the conversation. Micro-expressions—those fleeting facial movements that last only a fraction of a second—can also reveal true emotions. While they are often difficult to control, being aware of your facial expressions and practicing to keep them aligned with your verbal messages can go a long way in establishing trust.

Your gestures can further enhance your message if used appropriately. Hand movements can emphasize points and make your communication more dynamic. However, be mindful of your gestures, as exaggerated or erratic movements can be distracting or come off as anxious. A good rule of thumb is to keep gestures natural and in harmony with what you're saying. Controlled and purposeful use of your hands can make you appear more dynamic and engaged.

Beyond individual forms of body language, consider the overall alignment between your verbal and non-verbal communication. This alignment—or lack thereof—can make or break trust. Inconsistent messages can lead to confusion and skepticism. Practicing congruence between what you say and what you display ensures that your counterpart receives a clear, authentic message. For example, if you're expressing openness and flexibility verbally but have closed-off body language, your words lose their impact.

Let's not forget the power of mirroring. This technique involves subtly mimicking the other person's body language, gestures, and even tone of voice. Mirroring helps create a sense of familiarity and understanding, making the other person feel more at ease and connected to you. It's important to do this naturally and respectfully, as overt or mechanical mimicking can be easily detected and might be perceived as manipulative. When done right, however, mirroring can significantly enhance rapport and trust.

The tone and pace of your voice also play a massive role in non-verbal communication. A soft, calm tone can put the other party at ease, while a harsh or rapid tone might create tension or anxiety. Pay attention to the speed and rhythm of your speech. Speaking too quickly can make you seem nervous or overly aggressive, whereas speaking too slowly might come off as dull or condescending. Aim for a balanced pace that conveys confidence and competence.

Pauses are another underutilized yet powerful tool. Strategic pauses can give you time to think and can emphasize important points. They also show that you're considering the other party's input seriously. Such moments of silence can add weight to your words, making them more impactful. However, know when to employ them; overuse can make you seem hesitant or unsure.

While focusing on your own non-verbal cues is essential, paying attention to the other party's non-verbal signals is equally vital. Observing their body language, facial expressions, and gestures helps you gauge their feelings and reactions in real-time. Are they leaning in, nodding, and making eye contact? These signs typically indicate engagement and agreement. Conversely, crossed arms, lack of eye contact, or frequent glances at the clock might signal disengagement or discomfort. By reading these cues, you can adjust your approach accordingly, addressing concerns, and steering the conversation back on track.

Listening with your eyes is just as important as listening with your ears. When you notice the other person's non-verbal cues, you can respond in ways that show empathy and understanding. This creates a feedback loop of positive reinforcement, further solidifying the trust between both parties. For instance, if you notice the other person seems tense, do what you can to alleviate their stress. Perhaps a reassuring smile or a small gesture of understanding can make a difference.

For professionals keen to take their negotiation skills to the next level, understanding cultural differences in non-verbal communication is indispensable. In some cultures, direct eye contact is seen as respectful and confident, while in others, it might be considered confrontational. Similarly, gestures and body language have different meanings across cultures. A gesture that's positive in one culture may be offensive in another. Being aware of these nuances can prevent misunderstandings and foster smoother negotiations.

Arguably, self-awareness in non-verbal communication starts with practice and feedback. Engaging in role-playing exercises or recording your practice sessions can provide valuable insights into your own body language. You might be surprised to notice habits you were previously unaware of, such as frequently touching your face or avoiding eye contact. By becoming more mindful of your non-verbal cues, you can work on aligning them with your verbal messages to enhance trust and rapport.

Ultimately, non-verbal communication acts as the silent partner in negotiations. It can help build a bridge of trust or, if neglected, create an unintentional rift. Investing time in understanding and mastering this facet of communication offers a remarkable return. It enables you to connect more deeply with others, fostering trust that is essential for successful negotiations.

Establishing Credibility

When it comes to building rapport and trust in negotiations, establishing credibility is paramount. Without credibility, any attempt to connect or persuade becomes significantly harder. Think of credibility as the backbone of your negotiation persona.

The first step in establishing credibility is consistency. People tend to trust those who reliably do what they say they're going to do. This means being honest, following through on promises, and maintaining integrity throughout the process. If you commit to providing information by a certain date, ensure you deliver. Consistency in actions aligns with stated intentions and creates a foundation of trust.

Expertise also greatly enhances credibility. Demonstrating a deep understanding of the subject matter showcases your commitment and knowledge, which can translate to increased influence and trust. This means investing time in research and staying updated on relevant trends and developments. Expertise should not be flaunted; rather, it should be subtly woven into the dialogue to inform and guide the negotiation.

Another essential aspect is transparency. Being open about your intentions, motivations, and constraints helps in establishing credibility. This doesn't mean revealing every card in your hand but rather being straightforward about the aspects that you're comfortable sharing. Transparency fosters an environment where the other party feels safe to reciprocate, laying the groundwork for a two-way flow of honest communication.

Active listening plays a critical role as well. When you genuinely listen to the other party and actively engage with their concerns, you demonstrate respect and awareness, which in turn boosts your credibility. It shows that you are not merely pushing your agenda but are also invested in understanding and addressing their needs.

Moreover, acknowledging your limitations can be disarmingly effective. Pretending to know everything can backfire if you're caught out. Admitting what you don't know or where you lack expertise not only makes you more human but also more trustworthy. Authenticity in this regard can open doors to collaborative problem-solving.

Your network and affiliations also contribute to your credibility. Being associated with respected organizations or having endorsements from recognized experts can lend you an aura of trustworthiness. This form of social proof indicates that others value and believe in your capabilities, which can be incredibly persuasive.

Body language cannot be ignored. Non-verbal cues like maintaining eye contact, a firm but not overly aggressive handshake, and open postures communicate confidence and sincerity. These cues must align with your verbal communication to avoid sending mixed messages.

Ethical considerations are indispensable in maintaining credibility. Upholding high ethical standards not only feels right but also builds a reputation that precedes you. Acting ethically in all negotiations ensures long-term success and preserves relationships, which is often more valuable than individual transactions.

Establishing credibility is not an overnight task. It requires consistency, expertise, transparency, active listening, authenticity, social proof, confident body language, and a strong ethical foundation. By incorporating these elements, you can forge a powerful path toward trust and effective negotiation.

But let's dive a little deeper into some actionable strategies.

Firstly, document your achievements and share them selectively. Case studies, testimonials, or examples of past successes can go a long way in building your credibility. They serve as tangible proof of your experience and skills, making it easier for the other party to trust your abilities.

In parallel, providing value before the actual negotiation can set a positive tone. This could be in the form of insightful information, helpful suggestions, or even small favors that don't cost much but show your willingness to collaborate. Establishing this prelude creates a sense of goodwill and portrays you as a favorable partner.

Another crucial aspect is managing your reputation. Building credibility goes hand in hand with managing what others think and say about you. This means being mindful of your actions and words in every professional or social interaction. Be aware that your reputation can travel before you enter the negotiation room.

Preparation certainly helps, too. The more prepared you are, the more credible you'll appear. Knowing the facts, understanding the landscape, and being prepared for potential counterarguments enables you to present a well-rounded case, positioning yourself as someone who is serious and knowledgeable.

The ability to articulate your points clearly and confidently also strengthens credibility. Use facts, figures, and logical explanations to support your arguments. Avoid jargon unless you are absolutely sure that the other party understands it perfectly. Simplify complex ideas to make them more digestible.

Credibility also comes from showing respect. Respect the other party's time, emotions, and viewpoints. Simple gestures such as punctuality, being attentive, and valuing their input contribute to the overall perception of you as a credible negotiator.

Conceding points when appropriate can paradoxically strengthen your position. It shows that you're reasonable and willing to acknowledge valid points from the other side. This can make the other party more inclined to view your remaining positions as fair and worth considering.

Furthermore, using a collaborative approach can enhance credibility. Instead of a confrontational or adversarial mindset, aim to be a partner in problem-solving. This builds trust and shows that you're more interested in finding mutually beneficial solutions rather than purely advancing your interests.

Finally, avoid overpromising. It's tempting to say what the other party wants to hear, but it's far more sustainable to underpromise and overdeliver. This strategy builds long-lasting credibility because it consistently meets or exceeds expectations.

Given the complexity and dynamics of negotiation, establishing credibility is not a set-and-forget deal. It's an ongoing effort that requires vigilance, adaptability, and continued commitment to the principles outlined above. As you master these elements, you solidify a reputation as a formidable yet trustworthy negotiator.

And remember, credibility isn't solely about the immediate negotiation at hand. It's a long-term asset that will serve you across any professional interaction, contributing to lasting relationships and repeated successes.

Chapter 5: Strategies and Tactics

To navigate the complex world of negotiation, understanding the difference between strategies and tactics is essential. Strategies form the overarching plan, providing a roadmap for achieving long-term goals, while tactics are the specific actions employed at crucial moments to gain an advantage. Balancing competitive and collaborative approaches means not just focusing on winning, but also on creating mutually beneficial outcomes. Prioritizing your BATNA (Best Alternative to a Negotiated Agreement) and being aware of your ZOPA (Zone of Possible Agreement) can be game-changers. The art of concession-making involves giving ground wisely without losing your core objectives. By integrating these elements, you create a dynamic, flexible negotiation style that anticipates challenges and adapts to varied scenarios. Mastering the interplay of these strategies and tactics enables you to enter each negotiation as a calculated yet adaptive force, steering towards success with confidence and precision.

Competitive vs. Collaborative Approaches

When it comes to negotiation, there are generally two major strategies: competitive and collaborative approaches. Understanding these can make the difference between success and failure in any negotiation setting. Each has its own set of tactics, benefits, and drawbacks, and knowing when to employ either can give you a distinct edge.

Competitive negotiation is often likened to a zero-sum game, where one side's gain is another side's loss. Picture a pie that doesn't get any bigger;

if you take a bigger slice, someone else gets a smaller slice. This kind of strategy is usually marked by aggressive tactics such as high demands, limited concessions, and sometimes even bluffing. Competitive negotiators aren't shy about using power and leverage to get what they want—it's all about maximizing their own interests.

On the other hand, collaborative negotiation can be seen as a win-win scenario. The goal here is to expand the pie, so both parties walk away satisfied. Collaboration involves open communication, empathy, and a genuine effort to understand the other party's needs and interests. Think of it as a collective problem-solving endeavor where the focus is on mutual gains rather than individual victories.

Both approaches have their time and place, and the challenge lies in knowing which one to choose. For instance, in a high-stakes business deal where resources are scarce, a competitive approach might be more suitable. Conversely, when you're negotiating a long-term partnership or working on a project that requires ongoing cooperation, a collaborative approach is often more effective.

Employing a competitive approach effectively requires a deep understanding of power dynamics. One must be adept at identifying and exploiting leverage points. In essence, you're looking to tilt the scales in your favor at every opportunity. This doesn't just mean being the loudest voice in the room; it involves strategic planning, anticipating objections, and preparing counterarguments. You have to be ready to play hardball, but not recklessly so. The line between assertive and aggressive is thin, and crossing it can backfire.

In collaborative negotiation, emotional intelligence is crucial. You can't fake empathy and understanding; it has to be genuine. People are more inclined to cooperate if they feel heard and understood. Active listening becomes your greatest tool. When you validate the other party's concerns and work together to find solutions, you're building a foundation of trust and rapport. This kind of relationship is invaluable, particularly in negotiations that aim for long-term gains.

One of the most significant advantages of a collaborative approach is the preservation of relationships. When both parties walk away feeling like they've gained something, they're more likely to maintain a positive working relationship. This can lead to future opportunities and collaborations. By contrast, a competitive approach can strain relationships and lead to feelings of resentment, which might cost you in the long run.

That said, there are drawbacks to both strategies. Competitive negotiation can be mentally and emotionally exhausting. It requires a constant balancing act of assertiveness and diplomacy. Missteps can result in deadlocks and damaged relationships. Moreover, constantly using a competitive approach can build a reputation that might make others wary of negotiating with you in the future.

Collaborative negotiation, while generally more peaceful, isn't without its challenges. Being too accommodating can sometimes lead to suboptimal outcomes. There are instances where the other party may take advantage of your willingness to cooperate, resulting in a lopsided agreement. Striking the right balance between being cooperative and assertive is a skill that takes time to master.

So, how do you choose the right approach? It starts with thorough preparation. Knowing your own priorities and the other party's interests can guide your strategy. Ask yourself: What are the stakes? How much power do you hold, and what leverage points can you exploit? What's the nature of your relationship with the other party, and how will this negotiation affect it?

Another critical factor is flexibility. Sometimes, negotiations start competitively but can evolve into more collaborative discussions as mutual understanding grows. Staying adaptable and reading the room can give you the upper hand. Being rigid in your approach can lead to missed opportunities for mutually beneficial solutions.

Additionally, self-awareness plays a key role. Understand your natural tendencies and biases. Some people are naturally more competitive, while others are more inclined towards collaboration. Recognizing your own inclinations allows you to consciously adjust your strategy to suit the situation better.

When employing a competitive approach, it's essential not to overlook the human element. Negotiations aren't just about numbers and terms; they're about people. Even in the most cutthroat scenarios, a little empathy can go a long way. Knowing when to dial down the intensity and acknowledge the other party's concerns can prevent negotiations from going off the rails.

In collaborative settings, transparency and trust are paramount. However, transparency doesn't mean revealing all your cards right away. Strategic disclosure—sharing information that can foster trust without jeopardizing your position—is often the best route. Aim to create a dialogue where both parties feel safe to share their concerns and aspirations.

Let's take a look at some tactics for each approach. In competitive negotiation, anchoring is a commonly used tactic. It involves setting a reference point around which negotiations revolve. By making the first offer, you establish the "anchor" which can heavily influence the final outcome. Silence can also be a powerful tool. Sometimes, refusing to fill the void can pressure the other party to make concessions.

Collaborative tactics include brainstorming sessions where both parties actively contribute to finding solutions. Joint problem solving is another effective tactic, where you identify the issue at hand and work collaboratively to address it. Additionally, using 'what-if' scenarios can help explore various solutions without committing to any specific course of action.

Blending both strategies can sometimes yield the best results. Start with a competitive approach to set the stage, then gradually shift to collaborative tactics as the negotiation progresses. This allows you to anchor the discussion in your favor initially while still working towards a mutually beneficial outcome.

Ultimately, the key to mastering both competitive and collaborative approaches lies in continual learning and practice. Each negotiation is a new experience with different dynamics and variables. The more you engage, the better you'll become at recognizing which approach to use and when to switch gears.

In summary, competitive and collaborative approaches each have their own advantages and limitations. Knowing when and how to employ each strategy can significantly enhance your negotiation skills. Whether you're looking to clinch a high-stakes deal or build a long-lasting partnership, understanding these tactical approaches provides you with a toolkit for success in any negotiation scenario.

BATNA and ZOPA

In the grand theater of negotiation, understanding your BATNA and ZOPA is akin to knowing the plot and stage dimensions before the curtain rises. BATNA, or Best Alternative to a Negotiated Agreement, and ZOPA, or Zone of Possible Agreement, are two critical concepts that will empower you to navigate negotiations with precision and confidence.

Imagine BATNA as your safety net. It's your fallback option if the negotiation doesn't go as planned. Knowing your BATNA gives you the power to walk away from a deal that's not in your favor because you have an alternative. This element of preparation transforms an otherwise daunting "take-it-or-leave-it" scenario into a controlled environment where you hold the reins.

Consider a scenario where you're negotiating a contract with a client. If you know you have another client willing to offer you a similar or better deal, your BATNA strengthens your position. It emboldens you to push for better terms with your current client, ensuring you're not walking away from a negotiation with less than you deserve.

On the flip side, lacking a strong BATNA can put you in a precarious position. You're more likely to concede to unfavorable terms if you have no viable alternatives. Hence, a robust BATNA is not just a safety net; it's a potent weapon in your arsenal, allowing you to negotiate from a place of strength rather than desperation.

ZOPA, the Zone of Possible Agreement, is equally significant. It represents the range wherein both parties' interests overlap, providing the common ground required to reach an agreement. Understanding ZOPA necessitates a deep dive into both your own and the other party's needs, wants, and limits.

Thinking about the ZOPA helps in recognizing the dance space available for negotiation. For example, you want to buy a car and have a maximum budget of $20,000, while the seller's minimum acceptable price is $18,000. Your ZOPA is the range between $18,000 and $20,000. Armed with this knowledge, you can strategically work within this zone to craft a deal that satisfies both parties.

The magical confluence of BATNA and ZOPA lies in their dynamic interplay. An understanding of your BATNA clarifies your limits—where you can push and where you should retreat. Meanwhile, knowing the ZOPA ensures you're not overstepping bounds that would make an agreement impossible. Together, they navigate you through the fog of negotiation, highlighting pathways to a successful conclusion.

To further illustrate, let's dive into a narrative. Imagine a tech startup negotiating a partnership with a large corporation. The startup's BATNA could be pursuing venture capital funding if the partnership falls through. Knowing this, the startup can afford to push for more favorable revenue-sharing terms. If the corporation's BATNA is independently developing a similar technology (a costly and time-consuming alternative), the startup can glean insights into the likely ZOPA and negotiate within those boundaries.

However, it's not just about identifying BATNA and ZOPA; it's also about reframing them in light of new information. Negotiations are fluid. As discussions progress, new data can emerge, prompting a reassessment of both concepts. This adaptive strategy ensures you remain agile, enhancing your ability to respond to evolving circumstances.

During the negotiation process, it's crucial to ascertain the other party's BATNA as well. Understanding their fallback options provides a clearer perspective on their negotiation threshold. If their BATNA is weak, you have a larger strategic advantage. Conversely, if their BATNA is strong, it would be wise to tread carefully and recalibrate your expectations accordingly.

It's equally essential to recognize that BATNAs are not always static or obvious. They can evolve over time as new alternatives emerge or old ones vanish. A continuous re-evaluation of BATNA can lead to a more dynamic and informed negotiation strategy. Keep an ear to the ground and stay informed about external factors that might influence both your own and the other party's alternatives.

So, how do you practically integrate an understanding of BATNA and ZOPA into your negotiation strategy?

Firstly, thorough preparation is key. Invest time in researching potential alternatives before entering the negotiation. Know the landscape of options available to you. Whether it's alternative suppliers, different job offers, or other business partnerships, having this inventory empowers you to identify your best alternative with clarity.

Within the ZOPA framework, map out various scenarios. What are the extremes and what are the compromises? This exercise provides a range of possibilities, reinforcing your confidence and flexibility during the actual negotiation. You'll find yourself less rigid and more adaptable, capable of steering the discussion towards mutually beneficial outcomes.

It's worth noting that effective communication plays a pivotal role in enhancing your BATNA and ZOPA analysis. Engage in active listening and continually probe for information. Asking the right questions can uncover vital pieces of the puzzle, allowing you to adjust your strategy in real-time. Aim for transparency without giving away your strong suits too soon. Instead, strategically divulge information to progressively tilt the balance in your favor.

Let's bring it all together with an example from a high-stakes business negotiation. Suppose Company A is negotiating a merger with Company B. Company A's BATNA might be to merge with another smaller but financially sound company. Knowing this, Company A can confidently negotiate terms, knowing they have a solid fallback plan. Meanwhile, Company B's BATNA might be to continue operating independently, albeit less efficiently. Understanding this, Company A can fine-tune their offer to appeal to Company B's need for improving operational efficiency within the ZOPA, ensuring they strike a deal that's advantageous yet acceptable to both.

Ultimately, the principles of BATNA and ZOPA form the bedrock of strategic negotiations. They are not just academic concepts but practical tools that empower negotiators to navigate the complex interplay of interests, constraints, and opportunities. Whether you're hammering out a multi-million dollar business deal or negotiating a raise, these concepts grant you the clarity and confidence to achieve outcomes that not only meet but exceed your objectives.

Remember, a well-defined BATNA arms you with the strength to walk away, while an astutely identified ZOPA keeps you rooted in realistic possibilities.

Together, they don't just guide you; they guard you—ensuring that each negotiation you undertake is not just an exercise in compromise, but a strategic maneuver towards your goals.

The Art of Concession Making

In the labyrinthine world of negotiation, the ability to make concessions can be a powerful tool. Concession making is not just about giving in; it's about strategically yielding ground to gain a more advantageous position. It requires a deep understanding of timing, psychology, and the nuances of human behavior. By mastering the art of concession making, you can turn seemingly unfavorable situations into opportunities for mutual gain.

Concessions should never be made hastily or without adequate consideration. The first rule of thumb is to understand the value of what you're conceding and what you might gain in return. It's a delicate dance that involves offering something of lesser importance to you but of perceived value to the other party. This way, you create an atmosphere where both sides feel as if they've won something tangible.

Timing is another critical element. Knowing when to make a concession can often mean the difference between a successful negotiation and a missed opportunity. Early in negotiations, making a concession can be seen as a sign of weakness. However, as discussions advance, a well-timed concession can act as a goodwill gesture, paving the way for the other party to reciprocate. This establishes a balanced exchange and fosters a collaborative atmosphere.

Let's not forget the psychological underpinning of concessions. Humans are hardwired to respond favorably to reciprocity. When you make a concession, it often triggers a sense of obligation in the other party to do the same. This isn't just a theory; it's a well-documented principle in behavioral psychology. Utilizing this principle judiciously can create a virtuous cycle of give and take that propels negotiations forward.

The manner in which you make a concession also matters. It's essential to communicate its value clearly and to underscore what you expect in return. This way, you maintain control of the narrative and set the stage for the other party to view the concession as a fair exchange rather than a giveaway. For example, if you're negotiating a business deal, you might say, "We can agree to a lower price point if the payment terms are adjusted to net 30 days instead of net 60." This clarifies both what you're offering and what you're seeking, minimizing misunderstandings.

Keep in mind that smaller concessions can be just as significant as larger ones when strategically employed. Sometimes, small acts of flexibility can unlock significant gains. These micro-concessions might include adjusting meeting times, tweaking some minor terms in a contract, or even just showing more attentiveness to the other party's needs. These seemingly minute actions can build cumulative goodwill, making it easier to win larger concessions when they truly matter.

Awareness of the other party's needs and constraints can significantly strengthen your position. Conduct thorough research and find out what elements of the negotiation are non-negotiable for them and which areas have some wiggle room. By aligning your concessions with their lesser priorities, you can gain more in return. This might involve more than just listening during the negotiation; it could mean studying their past behaviors, understanding their business model, or even gathering intelligence through mutual connections.

Negotiation is also a test of patience. The urge to rush and close the deal can be overwhelming, particularly if deadlines loom large. However, hasty concessions often lead to regret and missed opportunities. Make sure that each concession is thoughtful and calculated, ensuring that it aligns with your overarching objectives.

Another useful tactic is to frame your concessions within a larger narrative. "Since we are committed to building a long-term relationship, we're willing to offer this initial discount." Framing it this way not only contextualizes your concession but also sets the expectation of future reciprocity. This narrative approach can be surprisingly effective in nudging the other party towards favorable decisions.

Transparency can be a double-edged sword in negotiations. While being open about your limits can generate empathy and trust, revealing too much can weaken your position. Strike a balance by being transparent about your motives without laying all your cards on the table. For instance, saying, "I can only increase our offer by five percent due to budget constraints," is more strategic than disclosing your maximum limit right away.

Even the tone and language you use can make a significant difference. Phrases like "We're willing to consider" or "Can we explore" suggest flexibility without conveying desperation. It's all about keeping the dialogue open and constructive, encouraging mutual problem-solving rather than adversarial posturing.

Of course, every negotiation has its own unique dynamics, and there are instances where hard-nosed tactics may require a firmer approach to concessions. In highly competitive settings, it might be crucial to stand your ground on key issues while offering non-critical concessions to maintain progress. What's important is to remain adaptable, reading the room and adjusting your strategy to the unfolding situation.

Lastly, it's worth mentioning the concept of "anchoring" in concession making. The initial conditions or offers set a psychological anchor that influences the entire negotiation trajectory. By making a strategic concession early, you can set a positive anchor, shifting the negotiation landscape favorably. For example, if you start negotiations with a slightly ambitious offer and then roll back to your ideal position, the other party might perceive this as a generous concession, making them more inclined to meet you halfway.

Mastering the art of concession making is an evolving process. It's more than just a tactic; it's a philosophy that involves understanding human psychology, leveraging timing, and perfecting the balance between giving and receiving. When executed skillfully, it can transform negotiations from combative exchanges into collaborative problem-solving sessions, leading to outcomes that are advantageous for everyone involved.

Chapter 6: Overcoming Obstacles

Y ou've mastered the strategies and built rapport, but challenges inevitably arise in any negotiation. This is the moment when true expertise shines. Overcoming obstacles is about harnessing your ability to remain calm and strategic under pressure. For instance, dealing with difficult people requires a delicate balance of empathy and firmness; recognize their concerns, but don't let them derail your objectives. Managing conflict and tension is equally critical—use your emotional intelligence to de-escalate situations, turning potential conflict into productive dialogue. When faced with deadlock, innovative techniques such as reframing issues or introducing new variables can break the stalemate. Remember, these obstacles test your skills, and every challenge is an opportunity to learn and improve, sharpening your ability to navigate even the most complex negotiations with grace and efficacy.

Dealing with Difficult People

Negotiating successfully often feels like choreography. Each step must be precise, the timing impeccable. But what happens when you encounter an unpredictable or difficult partner? They're the ones who refuse to yield, make outrageous demands, or use emotionally charged tactics to throw you off balance. Understanding how to deal with these challenging individuals is crucial to overcoming obstacles in negotiation.

First, it's important to recognize that difficult people often resort to specific behaviors because they're effective at throwing others off balance. They might interrupt frequently, talk over you, or alternate between aggressive and passive postures. These individuals thrive on emotional reactions, so maintaining your composure is key. When you keep calm, you can observe their tactics more clearly and plan your responses with a cool head.

Creating a buffer between your emotions and your actions can be a game-changer. Implementing pauses in the conversation allows you to gather your thoughts. Silence can also be a powerful tool in negotiation; it can make the difficult person uncomfortable and eager to fill the void. Let that pressure work to your advantage.

Next, assess your counterpart's motivations. Sometimes, difficult behavior stems from underlying fears or insecurities. Their aggressive stance might hide a lack of confidence, or perhaps they feel threatened by your position. By trying to understand their perspective, you gain valuable insight that can help diffuse tension. Empathy doesn't mean capitulation; it means you're looking to find a route to a mutually beneficial result.

Another effective strategy when dealing with difficult personalities is active listening. This technique involves really paying attention to what the other person is saying and then summarizing their points back to them. This not only confirms your understanding but also makes them feel heard. And when people feel heard, they're more likely to lower their defenses.

Now, consider setting boundaries. Clearly articulated limits on what's acceptable conduct can manage and mitigate difficult behaviors. For example, you might say, "I'm here to reach a solution that works for both of us, but we need to keep the discussion respectful." Often, this kind of direct approach can reset the tone of the conversation.

Difficult people often use manipulative tactics to get what they want. They might use guilt, outrage, or even charm to bend you to their will. Recognizing these maneuvers can help you neutralize them. In these situations, being assertive is crucial. Politely but firmly standing your ground demonstrates that you're neither intimidated nor easily swayed.

Let's not forget the importance of preparation. Knowledge is your greatest ally. Understanding the details of your negotiation inside and out leaves little room for difficult people to exploit. When you're well-prepared, you project confidence, making it harder for them to catch you off guard. Research your counterpart's business history, personal interests, and even previous negotiation styles if available.

While it's essential to have strategies prepared, adaptability cannot be overstated. Flexibility in your approach means you're prepared for any curveballs thrown your way. Think of it like a martial art: you're not rigid, but rather flow smoothly to counter and redirect negative energy. If the direct approach isn't working, consider shifting to a more collaborative style to build a bridge.

Humor can sometimes be a highly effective tool in de-escalating tense situations. A well-timed, light-hearted comment can break the ice and reset a heated conversation. However, it's important to gauge the appropriateness of humor carefully; a poorly timed joke can exacerbate tensions rather than relieve them.

Remember the "mirror technique"? It's a psychological tactic where you subtly mimic the body language and speech patterns of the other party. This can be particularly effective with difficult people as it creates a subtle rapport and lowers their defenses. People often respond more positively to interactions that feel familiar to them.

When dealing with tricky negotiators, setting the right tone from the beginning is crucial. Establishing ground rules and an agenda at the start of the meeting can prevent the conversation from derailing. This shows that you're serious and organized, which alone can discourage disruptive behavior.

Acknowledge and address the emotional undercurrents in the room. Ignoring the elephant in the room will only make it grow bigger. A simple statement like "I sense there's some frustration here, can we address that?" can pivot the discussion back to rational ground.

How about leveraging your network? Sometimes it's useful to bring a third party into the negotiation arena. This neutral party can act as a mediator, balancing out the intense dynamics between you and the difficult person.

It's also critical to manage your expectations. Not every negotiation will have a fairytale ending where everyone walks away happy. Accepting that a less-than-perfect deal might be necessary is part of becoming a master negotiator. The key is to weigh the long-term relationship against short-term wins.

Finally, never underestimate the power of the "walkaway." Knowing when to say, "This isn't beneficial for us, we'll have to leave it here," is an important tool in your arsenal. Declining to engage further when a situation is untenably difficult can sometimes lead to the other party recalibrating their approach, realizing they need you more than they initially thought.

By mastering these techniques, you empower yourself to handle even the most difficult negotiators with grace and effectiveness. The goal is not to overpower them, but to navigate through obstacles skillfully, emerging with an agreement that respects both your goals and theirs. Ultimately, this proficiency transforms the way you negotiate, making you a more formidable and respected presence at any negotiating table.

Managing Conflict and Tension

Conflict and tension are inevitable in any negotiation. They arise from opposing interests, miscommunications, and sometimes even from the pressure to succeed. While these challenges can be daunting, they also present opportunities for growth, learning, and potentially, for turning adversaries into allies. The key isn't to avoid conflict but to manage it wisely and constructively.

Consider a tense negotiation like navigating a storm. You can't control the weather, but you can control how you steer your ship. The first step in managing conflict is acknowledging it. Don't shy away from it, and don't pretend it isn't there. Instead, recognize its presence and understand its causes. This awareness is your compass, guiding you through the turbulent waters.

Understanding the root cause of conflict can often diffuse much of its intensity. Conflicts generally stem from unmet needs, unexpressed emotions, or misaligned goals. Engage in active listening to get to the heart of these issues. This involves more than just hearing words—it's about understanding the emotions and intentions behind them. Often, the simple act of feeling heard can significantly reduce tension.

Active listening is not just a skill; it's an art. Lean in, maintain eye contact, and use verbal nods to show you're engaged. Paraphrase what's being said to ensure clarity and show that you're genuinely trying to understand. For instance, you might say, "So, what I'm hearing is that you're concerned about the delivery timeline—am I correct?" This technique not only defuses the immediate tension but also builds a bridge of mutual respect.

Another crucial aspect is to manage your own emotions. Negotiations can be emotionally charged, but losing your cool can result in missed opportunities and damaged relationships. Take a moment to breathe and maintain your composure. Your ability to stay calm and collected will set the tone for the negotiation. It allows you to think more clearly and make more rational decisions.

Conflicts often escalate because of assumptions and misunderstandings. Clarify your intentions and be transparent about your objectives. This builds trust and can prevent minor disagreements from blowing up into major disputes. If the other party believes that you're hidden behind a veil of secrecy, they're more likely to meet you with resistance.

Transparency carries a level of vulnerability, but it also demonstrates confidence and integrity. By laying your cards on the table, you invite the other party to do the same. This openness can be disarming, encouraging a more honest and collaborative atmosphere. It's not about showing all your hand, but about communicating your intentions clearly and honestly.

Utilize the power of *collaborative problem-solving*. Approach conflicts not as battles to be won, but as puzzles to be solved together. Shift the focus from positions to interests. Instead of getting hung up on what each side wants, explore why they want it. This deeper understanding can uncover common ground and create opportunities for mutually beneficial solutions.

Conflicts are also excellent opportunities to demonstrate empathy. Put yourself in the other party's shoes and try to see the situation from their perspective. This can soften their stance and make them more amenable to compromise. Empathy doesn't mean agreement, but it shows that you respect their feelings and viewpoints.

Sometimes, despite your best efforts, conflict and tension can reach a boiling point. This is where adopting a strategy of tactical retreat can be invaluable. Take a break, give everyone time to cool off, and come back to the table with a fresh perspective. Pausing the negotiation isn't a sign of weakness; it's a strategic move to prevent rash decisions.

In some cases, bringing in a neutral third party can help mediate the discussion. A mediator can provide an unbiased perspective and help both parties see the bigger picture. They can facilitate a dialogue, ensuring that the negotiation remains productive and does not devolve into unproductive arguments.

Mediation does more than just resolve the immediate conflict; it can also provide insights into how similar issues can be handled in the future. It's a form of constructive feedback loop, offering learning experiences for all parties involved. By recognizing patterns and understanding triggers, you can better prepare for and manage future negotiations.

Additionally, establishing ground rules for communication can be beneficial. Agree to a set of norms, such as no interrupting, maintaining a respectful tone, and avoiding personal attacks. These guidelines can keep the discussion on track and ensure that it remains focused and civil. Sometimes, the environment in which negotiation takes place can also influence the outcome. A neutral, comfortable setting can ease tensions and foster a more open dialogue.

Empower your negotiation with a mindset of flexibility. Rigidity tends to escalate tension while flexibility can diffuse it. Be open to alternative solutions and creative compromises. Adaptability shows that you are more focused on reaching a resolution that works for both parties rather than sticking to a preconceived notion of success.

Conflict in negotiation is inevitable but manageable. The art lies in converting disagreements into open dialogue. By practicing active listening, maintaining emotional control, and being transparent and empathetic, you can navigate through tension-filled discussions effectively. Approach each conflict as an opportunity to learn and grow, both as a negotiator and as a person. Remember, the goal is not just to win but to foster an environment where all parties feel respected and heard.

Conflicts don't just test your negotiation skills; they also reveal your character. In heated moments, your true self emerges. Allow these moments to showcase your integrity, patience, and willingness to understand. By managing conflict and tension adeptly, you don't just reach agreements—you create lasting, positive relationships that are crucial for long-term success.

Techniques for Breaking Deadlocks

In the often tumultuous terrain of negotiation, deadlocks are almost inevitable. But a stalemate doesn't mean the end of the road. Innovative techniques and strategic maneuvers can break through these impasses, transforming deadlocks into mutual agreements. These techniques don't just require skill; they demand an understanding of human psychology, emotional intelligence, and a sound knowledge of negotiation dynamics.

Understanding why a deadlock occurs is crucial. It could stem from rigid positions, unmet underlying interests, or miscommunication. Recognizing the root cause allows you to address the core issue rather than the symptoms. For instance, a seemingly immovable stance might hide unvoiced concerns or fears. Uncovering these through open-ended questions can soften their rigidity.

One effective technique is to reframe the negotiation. When discussions stagnate, changing the narrative or context can open up new perspectives. Instead of pushing against a wall, think of how you can pivot. You can focus on shared goals, like long-term benefits or mutual risks, to shift the conversation from positions to interests. Breaking out of the zero-sum mindset reveals opportunities for creative solutions.

Flexibility is key. Sometimes, a rigid stance is due to a lack of perceived alternatives. Introducing new variables into the negotiation can create room for maneuver. This might involve adding, subtracting, or modifying terms. For example, if the price is non-negotiable, could the payment terms be adjusted, or could non-monetary benefits be included? Think outside the proverbial box.

Another powerful approach is the 'Yes, And' technique. Instead of countering a position with "No, but," respond with "Yes, and." This not only validates the other party's point but also redirects the conversation towards a joint problem-solving endeavor. Imagine someone saying, "We need a 10% discount to proceed." Instead of outright refusal, counter with, "Yes, and if we agree on a long-term partnership, we could discuss additional savings." This technique fosters a collaborative spirit.

Additionally, introducing a third-party mediator can be game-changing. A neutral party often brings fresh perspectives and can facilitate dialogue where direct negotiation falters. Mediators aren't just neutral; they are skilled in conflict resolution, enabling both sides to see beyond personal biases and emotional blocks.

Pausing the negotiation process can be surprisingly effective. Allowing time for reflection can enable both sides to reconsider their positions. When tensions are high, stepping back provides a breather. This isn't a sign of defeat but rather a strategic retreat, signaling maturity and patience. Often, the passage of time brings new insights and reduced emotional charge.

Another method to consider is building smaller agreements within the larger negotiation. These quick wins create positive momentum. By accumulating small victories, trust builds, and both parties feel a sense of progress. This can break down larger issues into more manageable components, encouraging a cooperative atmosphere. It's akin to assembling a puzzle piece by piece rather than forcing the parts together.

Techniques like the "What-If" scenario can also be fruitful. Engage in a hypothetical discussion to explore potential resolutions. "What if we extended the project deadline? What if we included a performance bonus?" Such questions encourage out-of-the-box thinking and break the rigidity of entrenched positions. This approach often reveals overlooked opportunities and solutions.

Don't underestimate the power of active listening. Often, deadlocks are exacerbated by a lack of understanding. Employing active listening techniques, such as paraphrasing the other party's points, can clarify misunderstandings and show genuine interest. When the other party feels heard and understood, they are more likely to reciprocate, fostering a conducive atmosphere for breakthrough.

Harnessing empathy is another valuable technique. Understanding the emotional and psychological needs of the other party can shift the dynamics. Sometimes, the deadlock isn't about the tangible terms but the need for respect, acknowledgment, or validation. Addressing these emotional undercurrents can dissolve barriers that seemed insurmountable.

Consider the chess analogy. In chess, sometimes a bold, unexpected move can change the game's direction. Similarly, in negotiation, introducing an unconventional proposal can surprise and open up new pathways. This isn't about being reckless but rather calculated creativity. It might involve proposing a partnership, joint venture, or innovative business model that wasn't initially on the table.

Interpersonal dynamics play a crucial role in breaking deadlocks. Building personal rapport and trust can ease the tension and open up lines of communication. Sharing a meal or a casual conversation outside the formal negotiation setting can humanize both parties, transforming adversaries into collaborators. Small gestures of goodwill, like acknowledging a good point or showing genuine concern for mutual interests, can have a substantial impact.

Sometimes, involving higher-level executives or decision-makers can propel the negotiation forward. These individuals might have the authority to adjust terms and provide new perspectives. They can transcend departmental or functional priorities, looking at the bigger picture, thus facilitating breakthroughs.

Balancing assertiveness with empathy is essential. While standing firm on critical issues, understanding and addressing the other party's concerns show emotional intelligence. This dual approach can soften the adversarial stance and create an environment where both sides feel respected and valued.

Remember, breaking a deadlock often requires patience and persistence. The process might be slow, but it's essential to keep the long-term objectives in sight. Every step, no matter how small, can inch you closer to a resolution. Maintain optimism and keep exploring avenues.

Providing a choice can also break the deadlock. Instead of presenting a single proposal, offer multiple options. This technique empowers the other party, providing them with a sense of control and involvement. It also subtly shifts the focus from rejection to selection, opening up new possibilities for agreement.

Finally, always circle back to the why. Reiterate the overarching goals and benefits of reaching an agreement. Sometimes, the minutiae eclipse the bigger picture. Reminding both parties of the end goal can reignite the shared vision and drive towards finding common ground.

Breaking deadlocks is not just about strategy; it's an art that blends psychology, empathy, patience, and creativity. By employing these techniques, you can navigate through the seemingly impenetrable walls of conflict, turning deadlocks into opportunities for meaningful agreements.

Chapter 7: Real-Life Case Studies

T hroughout our journey in mastering negotiation, understanding the theory is invaluable, but real-life examples bring those principles to life. Consider the high-stakes acquisition of a tech startup: one company recognized the strategic alignment and potential for market expansion, aligning their offer with both financial incentives and the target company's vision. This created a win-win situation where both parties felt valued and respected. Similarly, reflecting on a major retailer's failed negotiations with a supplier reveals how neglecting cultural considerations and underestimating the supplier's leverage led to a missed opportunity and strained relations. These anecdotes underscore the importance of empathy, thorough preparation, and strategic flexibility. By dissecting the triumphs and pitfalls, we can distill actionable insights and weave these lessons into our negotiation toolkit, enhancing our ability to navigate future challenges with confidence and finesse.

Successful Negotiations in Business

Successful negotiations in business are more than just an exercise in attaining mutual benefit; they're a testament to how preparation, strategy, and a firm grasp of psychology can yield remarkable outcomes. Take the negotiation between Apple and AT&T for the first iPhone, for instance. Apple wanted to revolutionize the smartphone market while maintaining strict control over its product and user experience. AT&T saw an opportunity to introduce a groundbreaking service and significantly boost market share. The result was a win-win agreement that became a turning point in the telecommunications industry.

Consider the significance of preparation and research, as demonstrated by this case. Apple's meticulous planning and understanding of both its needs and AT&T's incentives paved the way for a partnership that seemed almost impossible at the outset. Steve Jobs, Apple's CEO at the time, was relentless in his vision and unwavering in his demands. He didn't just rely on hunches; his team did an extensive analysis of market trends, customer desires, and the competitive landscape. This in-depth preparation meant that when Jobs sat down at the negotiating table, he was armed with compelling data and a clear vision, making it difficult for AT&T to say no.

In another high-stakes negotiation, we can look at the partnership between Starbucks and PepsiCo. Starbucks was seeking to extend its brand into the ready-to-drink coffee market, and PepsiCo was looking for a premium product to bolster its portfolio. By focusing on collaborative strategies, both parties leveraged their respective strengths. Starbucks brought its brand and coffee expertise, while PepsiCo contributed its extensive distribution network. The negotiations resulted in the formation of the North American Coffee Partnership, a venture that's still thriving today.

This case highlights the power of collaboration over competition. Both companies understood that by working together, they could achieve far more than by attempting to go it alone. Instead of viewing each other as competitors vying for market dominance, they saw an opportunity to create a complementary relationship. The Starbucks-PepsiCo deal exemplifies how identifying and aligning mutual interests can foster sustainable, long-term success.

Let's not forget the importance of emotional intelligence in negotiation, vividly illustrated by the Microsoft-LinkedIn deal. When Microsoft acquired LinkedIn for $26.2 billion, it wasn't just about the money. Satya Nadella, CEO of Microsoft, demonstrated a keen understanding of LinkedIn's culture and values, reassuring LinkedIn's leadership that their unique identity would be preserved post-acquisition. This empathy and respect for the other party's perspective turned potential friction into smooth sailing.

Not every negotiation, however, is smooth or straightforward. Consider the Walt Disney Company's acquisition of 21st Century Fox. It was a complex, prolonged affair involving regulatory hurdles, bidding wars with Comcast, and numerous other challenges. Yet, Disney's leadership navigated these obstacles by staying focused on their strategic objectives: expanding their content library and streaming capabilities. They kept their eyes on the prize, using patience and strategic concessions——such as agreeing to sell certain assets to alleviate antitrust concerns——to eventually close the deal.

Analyzing the Disney case, one can see that successful business negotiations often require adaptability and resilience. Regulatory challenges could have derailed the entire acquisition, but Disney's ability to reassess and adapt its approach was crucial. Moreover, being willing to make strategic concessions showed that flexibility can be an asset, not a weakness.

Consider the case of Amazon and Whole Foods. When Amazon sought to enter the grocery business, it faced skepticism from consumers and industry experts alike. However, through astute negotiation, they convinced Whole Foods of the synergistic benefits. Amazon assured Whole Foods of operational autonomy while promising improvements through its technological prowess. The result? A $13.7 billion deal that redefined the retail grocery landscape.

It's critical to recognize that in business, negotiations often extend beyond the boardroom. The real work begins when the ink dries. The Amazon–Whole Foods acquisition changed more than just ownership; it brought about significant operational and cultural shifts. Amazon leveraged its technological expertise to revolutionize Whole Foods' supply chain and customer experience, creating a symbiosis that went far beyond the initial negotiation table.

In the world of mergers and acquisitions, the powerhouse negotiation between Facebook and Instagram stands out. Facebook's acquisition of Instagram for $1 billion is often cited as a textbook example of understanding market potential. Instagram, with its rapidly growing user base, was poised to become a formidable competitor. By acquiring Instagram, Facebook didn't just gain a popular app; it also acquired a user base that would fuel its own growth. Mark Zuckerberg's foresight and strategic vision ensured that Facebook remained at the forefront of social media innovation.

Yet, the negotiation wasn't just about numbers. Zuckerberg's approach involved building a rapport with Instagram's founders, understanding their vision, and ensuring they felt valued even as part of a larger company. This respect and alignment of vision played a crucial role in sealing the deal.

Another compelling example is the negotiation that led to the collaboration between Tesla and Panasonic. Tesla, known for its electric vehicles, needed a reliable supplier of high-quality batteries to meet its ambitious production goals. Panasonic, on the other hand, sought to strengthen its foothold in the burgeoning electric vehicle market. The resulting partnership led to the construction of the Gigafactory, a colossal battery manufacturing facility that has helped both companies advance their respective positions in the market.

The Tesla-Panasonic negotiation underscores the importance of long-term thinking. Elon Musk, CEO of Tesla, didn't just negotiate for immediate gains; he envisioned a future where both companies could grow symbiotically. This forward-thinking approach allowed for a partnership that has continually evolved and delivered value far beyond the initial agreement.

Examining these real-life case studies reveals common threads. Successful negotiators prepare meticulously, understand the psychology of their counterparts, build genuine rapport, stay adaptable, and always keep sight of the long-term vision. These elements, when combined, create a framework that can turn even the most challenging negotiations into remarkable success stories.

In the rapidly changing landscape of business, the art of negotiation is a critical skill that can make or break deals. Whether it's a multi-billion dollar acquisition, a strategic partnership, or a market entry initiative, understanding the principles of successful negotiations can empower business professionals and entrepreneurs to secure deals that propel their organizations to new heights. Embracing these lessons from some of the most successful business negotiations provides a practical roadmap for anyone looking to master this vital skill.

In every negotiation, there's a delicate balance of power, perception, and persuasion at play. Learning from these real-life successes equips us with the tools to influence outcomes in our favor, leaving all parties feeling like winners. And that, ultimately, is the hallmark of a truly successful business negotiation.

Lessons from Failed Negotiations

Failure in negotiations doesn't just leave a sour taste—it's a goldmine of valuable lessons. With the right perspective, even the most disastrous negotiation experiences can be your best teacher. One might think that failed negotiations only lead to tangible losses like money or missed opportunities; however, the hidden costs, such as damaged relationships, wasted time, and bruised reputations, can often outweigh immediate losses.

Still, examining what went wrong offers profound insights. Take, for example, the ill-fated merger talks between AOL and Time Warner. At the time, it seemed like a match made in heaven. AOL was riding high on the dot-com bubble, and Time Warner was an established giant with a rich media portfolio. The deal was announced with much fanfare, but soon the cracks began to show. AOL's stock value plummeted, turning what was supposed to be the "deal of the century" into an abject disaster. The principal lesson? Overestimating your position and undervaluing the synergy required can result in catastrophic failures.

One crucial takeaway is the importance of realistic appraisals. Over-optimistic projections can skew expectations and lead to colossal disappointments. In AOL-Time Warner's case, executives failed to account for the cultural clash between a fast-paced tech company and a traditional media conglomerate. This highlighted the need to align not just financial interests but also corporate cultures.

Humility in negotiations can often be the antidote to hubris. Chess legend Garry Kasparov famously noted how arrogance can lead to downfall—a lesson equally applicable in negotiation rooms. The airline pricing war between American Airlines and Braniff Airways in the early 1980s serves as an example. Braniff attempted to undercut American's fares, thinking price slashing would capture market share swiftly. Yet, American Airlines had a better grasp of their cost structure and launched the "Super Saver" fares. Braniff couldn't keep up financially and eventually filed for bankruptcy. The lesson here? Know your limits and your competitor's capabilities thoroughly.

A common pitfall in negotiations is ignoring the importance of preparation. The 1985 summit between U.S. President Ronald Reagan and Soviet General Secretary Mikhail Gorbachev in Reykjavik serves as a historical lesson. What was supposed to be an unparalleled opportunity to ease Cold War tensions fell apart due to unaddressed preparatory details and misaligned priorities. While the two leaders managed to build rapport, they lacked concrete agreements on critical issues, leading to a stalemate.

Preparation isn't just about gathering data; it's about being ready for potential roadblocks. Make comprehensive checklists, identify your absolute deal-breakers, and genuinely understand the other party's pain points. Failing to do so might lead to missed opportunities, no matter how promising things initially seem.

Another key lesson from failed negotiations is understanding the emotional landscape. Consider the failed negotiations between the NFL and the NFL Players Association in 2011. Initially, both sides postured aggressively, with each party wanting to secure a larger share of revenue. Emotions ran high, and neither side was willing to make the first move towards compromise. The result? A labor lockout that lasted months, costing millions of dollars. Eventually, the situation was resolved, but the emotional damage and mistrust lingered for a long time.

Emotional intelligence in negotiations cannot be overstated. Recognizing when emotions are running high and knowing how to de-escalate can be more crucial than the actual terms on the table. Use techniques like active listening, empathy, and even strategic silence to understand and mitigate emotional barriers. The human element often underlies what externally seems purely transactional.

The 2019 breakdown of Brexit negotiations between the United Kingdom and the European Union revealed another critical aspect—timing. The UK's push to expedite the deal led to hurried decisions that didn't sit well with the EU's more cautious, detail-oriented approach. Rushed timelines often lead to shortcuts, misunderstandings, and half-baked agreements. It's a classic case where the need for speed overshadowed the necessity for precision.

We also learn the value of clear communication from these breakdowns. Enron's failed negotiations with Dynegy in 2001 showed how lack of transparency can derail even the most promising deals. Enron's financial troubles were much worse than what they disclosed, leading Dynegy to back out. The consequences were dire, not just for Enron but for all stakeholders involved. Transparency fosters trust, and trust facilitates successful negotiations.

The missed opportunity for the New York Yankees to sign Hall of Famer Reggie Jackson offers another anecdotal lesson. Jackson was keen to join the Yankees, but the team's management failed to recognize his value and didn't approach the negotiation table with a compelling offer initially. It was only later, after lots of back-and-forth and lost goodwill, that the Yankees secured Jackson. The hesitation and lack of initial appreciation almost cost them a legendary talent.

For anyone involved in negotiations, it's crucial to seize the moment. Understand the value you bring, as well as the value the other party can potentially offer. Delays and indecisiveness can erode opportunities, sometimes irreversibly. A decisive mindset coupled with thorough research can help you strike while the iron is hot.

Loyalty programs between retailers and customers illustrate the importance of sustaining relationships beyond the initial agreement. Many businesses focus so much on closing the deal that they neglect continued engagement, leading to customer attrition. For instance, when Starbucks initially launched their loyalty program, it faced criticism and lagging participation rates because the terms were too complicated. Simplicity and clarity won in the end, but only after learning from their mistakes and adjusting their strategy.

Strategic follow-through is key. The negotiation doesn't end when the deal is signed. Constantly nurture the relationship to adapt to evolving needs and solidify long-term success. Post-negotiation strategies should never be overlooked if you're aiming for enduring relationships and sustained value.

In summary, failed negotiations can be a treasure trove of wisdom if we're willing to glean the lessons they offer. From misalignment of interests, inadequate preparation, and emotional mismanagement, to poor timing, lack of transparency, indecisiveness, and neglect of post-deal relationships—each facet of failure is an opportunity to grow. Mastering negotiation is a journey, where each step, including the missteps, teaches invaluable skills that sharpen your acumen and broaden your understanding.

Key Takeaways

Real-life case studies illustrate the practical application of negotiation theories and provide invaluable lessons for business professionals and entrepreneurs. Here are the key takeaways:

- **Preparation is Crucial:** Successful negotiations, such as Apple's deal with AT&T, emphasize the importance of meticulous planning and understanding both your needs and your counterpart's incentives.
- **Focus on Collaboration:** The Starbucks and PepsiCo partnership shows that aligning mutual interests and leveraging respective strengths can lead to sustainable, long-term success.
- **Emotional Intelligence Matters:** The Microsoft-LinkedIn deal highlights how empathy and respect for the other party's perspective can turn potential friction into a smooth collaboration.
- **Adaptability and Resilience:** Disney's acquisition of 21st Century Fox demonstrates the need to stay focused on strategic objectives and be willing to make concessions to navigate regulatory challenges and other obstacles.
- **Strategic Vision:** The Amazon-Whole Foods and Facebook-Instagram deals underscore the importance of long-term thinking and understanding market potential to seize opportunities and drive innovation.
- **Building Rapport:** Successful negotiators, like Mark Zuckerberg with Instagram's founders, build genuine connections and ensure all parties feel valued to secure mutually beneficial agreements.
- **Long-Term Partnerships:** The Tesla-Panasonic negotiation shows the value of envisioning a symbiotic future where both parties can grow together, leading to ongoing, evolving partnerships.

- **Learn from Failures:** Examining failed negotiations reveals the importance of realistic appraisals, thorough preparation, emotional intelligence, and maintaining clear communication to avoid pitfalls and capitalize on lessons learned.
- **Importance of Timing:** The Brexit negotiations and other failed deals highlight that rushed timelines can lead to shortcuts and misunderstandings, emphasizing the need for precision over speed.
- **Transparency Fosters Trust:** Cases like Enron's failed negotiations with Dynegy demonstrate that lack of transparency can derail promising deals, reinforcing the value of honesty in building trust.
- **Seize Opportunities Decisively:** The New York Yankees' hesitant approach with Reggie Jackson shows that indecisiveness can erode opportunities, making it crucial to strike decisively when the moment is right.
- **Post-Deal Relationship Management:** Effective follow-through, as seen in loyalty programs, is essential for nurturing long-term success and adapting to evolving needs.

These insights from real-life case studies provide a practical roadmap for mastering negotiation skills. By learning from both successes and failures, professionals can enhance their ability to navigate future challenges with confidence and achieve remarkable outcomes.

Chapter 8: Cross-Cultural Negotiations

Engaging in cross-cultural negotiations can feel like embarking on a journey into uncharted territories, where both the map and the language require close scrutiny. Understanding and appreciating cultural differences is crucial, as these variations influence personal values, communication styles, and negotiation tactics. Strategies that work seamlessly in one culture might falter in another, causing unexpected friction or misunderstandings. It's not just about knowing that there are differences, but how to navigate them effectively. By incorporating empathy, patience, and a deep respect for the nuances of each culture, you can turn potential stumbling blocks into stepping stones. Grasping the concept of ethnocentrism – the belief in the superiority of one's own culture – is paramount. Recognize its risks and strive to view situations from multiple cultural perspectives. This openness fosters mutual respect and paves the way for more meaningful and successful negotiations across borders. Mastering cross-cultural negotiation isn't just an asset; it's a powerful catalyst for building international relationships that thrive on diversity and mutual understanding.

Cultural Differences and Their Impact

Imagine walking into a negotiation, not completely sure what to expect because the other party is from a culture vastly different from your own. You're not just negotiating terms; you're navigating an intricate web of values, social cues, and expectations. That's the reality of cross-cultural negotiations, where understanding cultural differences isn't just a nicety—it's a necessity.

To grasp the true impact of cultural differences, let's talk about communication styles. In high-context cultures, such as Japan or China, much of the communication is implicit. The words themselves are only part of the message; body language, tone, and context fill in the gaps. On the other end of the spectrum, you have low-context cultures like the United States and Germany, where clarity and directness are highly valued. Misinterpreting these signals can derail negotiations before they even begin.

Consider an example: You're an American negotiating with a Japanese company. You might assume that a nod means agreement. In reality, it could simply be a gesture indicating attentiveness, not necessarily concurrence. If you press forward thinking you've reached consensus, you might find yourself unpleasantly surprised down the line when the agreement falls through.

Time orientation also plays a critical role. Cultures differ in their approach to time—whether they see it as linear and scarce or more fluid and abundant. In western cultures, punctuality is often seen as a sign of respect. Meetings are scheduled strictly, and deadlines are sacred. Contrast this with some Middle Eastern or African cultures, where relationships might take precedence over timeliness. Being late isn't necessarily a sign of disrespect, but rather an acceptance that events unfold in their own time. Misunderstand these nuances, and you might appear rude or impatient, damaging rapport.

Next, factor in the cultural attitudes towards hierarchy and authority. In egalitarian cultures like those in Scandinavia, everyone in a team might have a say in the negotiation process. Consensus is the goal, and decisions are often made collaboratively. This is starkly different from more hierarchical cultures, such as those in India or Mexico, where decisions are typically made by top executives and deference to seniority is expected. Understanding these dynamics can help you identify the real decision-makers and streamline the negotiation process.

Let's not overlook the importance of relationship-building. In many cultures, trust and rapport aren't built overnight or through a single meeting. Southern European and Latin American cultures, for instance, place substantial value on relationship-building, often preferring to do business with people they know well. This can mean multiple meetings, shared meals, and genuine connections before any business talk begins. In contrast, in many Western cultures, getting straight to the point is sometimes appreciated, and focusing on the transaction might take precedence over relationship-building.

Another angle worth considering is the negotiation style preferred in different cultures. Americans are often known for their assertive, competitive approach, aiming for the best possible deal. On the flip side, the Japanese might prefer a more harmonious, consensus-driven approach, aiming for a win-win outcome. Navigating these differences requires adaptability and a deep understanding of the other party's cultural background.

Now, let's dive into how these cultural nuances play out in real terms. Take the case of two multinational corporations—one based in Germany and the other in Brazil. The German company is well-organized and detail-oriented, preparing meticulously for each meeting. Agendas and timelines are rigid. Their Brazilian counterparts, however, may have a more flexible approach, seeing the negotiation process as a dynamic interaction where improvisation isn't just acceptable, but expected.

In such scenarios, it's not just important to know these cultural traits; it's crucial to respect them. The German team might benefit from loosening their tightly-held schedules and allowing for some spontaneity. Meanwhile, the Brazilian team could recognize the value their German counterparts place on structure and try to align without compromising their fluid style. The magic lies in finding balance—a middle ground where both parties feel respected and heard.

Remember, adaptability is your most valuable tool. Flexibility in your approach can make a world of difference. Start negotiations with an open mind, willing to adapt your style and tactics based on the cultural context. It's not just about being courteous; it's about being strategically agile.

But strategies alone aren't enough. You also need emotional intelligence to read the room accurately and respond appropriately. This means being attuned to non-verbal cues that might indicate discomfort, enthusiasm, or confusion. Sometimes a smile or a nod offers more insight than spoken words.

With emotional intelligence also comes the skill of active listening. Too often, negotiators are so focused on their objectives that they miss subtle cues and underlying concerns from the other party. Active listening involves asking open-ended questions, paraphrasing for clarity, and showing genuine empathy. This not only builds trust but also gives you deeper insights into the true priorities and reservations of your counterparts.

Let's also consider the role of cultural etiquette in negotiations. Simple gestures like greetings, gift-giving, and even attire can hold different meanings across cultures. In some Asian cultures, presenting a business card with both hands is a sign of respect, while in the Middle East, discussing business over a meal is commonplace. Missteps here can lead to unintended offense or awkwardness, so researching these aspects before entering into negotiations is crucial.

Another fascinating aspect of cross-cultural negotiations involves decision-making processes. In some cultures, decisions are made quickly and independently, while in others, they require consultation with various stakeholders. For instance, an American executive might make a quick decision after a brief discussion, whereas a Japanese counterpart might need time to consult with their team and reach a group consensus.

Here's a quick tip: when negotiating with counterparts from collaborative cultures, be prepared for slower decision-making processes. Offer timelines that give them ample opportunity to consult and deliberate. Conversely, if you're dealing with a culture that values swift decisions, be ready to present concise, well-structured information to facilitate faster agreement.

Navigating these complexities isn't easy, but the rewards are substantial. Once you master the art of cross-cultural negotiation, you open up opportunities that others might shy away from. You'll be able to form alliances, enter new markets, and build partnerships that transcend cultural boundaries.

In conclusion, cultural differences significantly impact negotiation strategies, styles, and outcomes. By understanding and respecting these differences, you become a more effective, empathetic, and successful negotiator. Employ strategies tailored to fit the diverse cultural backgrounds of your counterparts, and you're more likely to reach mutually beneficial outcomes.

The next step in your journey involves specific strategies for navigating these global negotiations. In our upcoming section, we'll delve into techniques and tools that can further refine your cross-cultural negotiation prowess. Stay tuned, as we're just getting started.

Strategies for Global Negotiations

Global negotiations are an intricately choreographed dance, blending together different cultures, perspectives, and expectations. When you're stepping onto this international stage, an appreciation of the nuances becomes the key to unlocking successful deals. It's not just about speaking the same language; it's about understanding the worldview of your counterpart.

The first strategy to master is cultural sensitivity. Every culture has its own set of customs, traditions, and social norms that profoundly influence their approach to negotiation. Some cultures value directness and efficiency, while others prioritize relationship-building and subtlety. Navigating these waters requires a deep understanding of the cultural backdrop. For instance, in Japan, the concept of "saving face" is paramount, meaning that direct confrontation or making someone look bad in front of others could severely damage the negotiation process.

Next, recognize the importance of building personal relationships. In many cultures, particularly in Latin America and the Middle East, negotiations are less transactional and more relational. Deals often hinge on personal connections and the trust that accompanies them. Investing time in relationship-building activities, such as sharing meals or attending social events, can create a strong foundation for successful negotiations. Authentic engagement is crucial—superficiality can be quickly recognized and may backfire.

Then, there's the critical skill of active listening. It goes beyond merely hearing words; it's about understanding the underlying messages, emotions, and intentions. In cross-cultural settings, active listening helps you decode what's not being said as much as what's vocalized. By demonstrating genuine interest and understanding, you build trust and open the doors for more transparent communication.

Adaptability is another cornerstone. Different cultures have different preferences when it comes to negotiation styles. Some may prefer a linear, structured approach, while others thrive in more fluid, dynamic interactions. Be prepared to shift your strategy to align with your counterpart's preferred mode of operation. This flexibility not only facilitates smoother interactions but also showcases respect and consideration.

One cannot underestimate the power of doing thorough homework. Before entering any negotiation, substantial research into the cultural norms, business etiquette, and negotiation styles of the other party is essential. This preparation can include learning about their holidays, dress codes, and gestures—which in some cultures, a simple hand gesture can have vastly different meanings. Armed with this knowledge, you can avoid unintentional faux pas that could derail the entire negotiation process.

Language barriers can pose significant challenges. While it's ideal to have a common language, sometimes that's just not possible. The use of interpreters can be beneficial, but it's vital to choose one who's not only fluent in both languages but also adept at the cultural nuances. Misinterpretation can easily occur if the subtleties of language and context aren't fully captured. An experienced interpreter can bridge the gap and ensure both sides are accurately understood.

In addressing the pace of negotiations, be mindful that time perception varies across cultures. Western cultures tend to view time as a finite resource and favor swift negotiations, whereas many Asian and Middle Eastern cultures might see patience and thoroughness as virtues in the negotiation process. Rushing these parties can be interpreted as disrespectful, potentially jeopardizing the deal.

Furthermore, understanding the decision-making hierarchy within different cultures can prevent missteps. In some cultures, decisions are made collectively, requiring consensus from multiple stakeholders. In others, a single leader may have the authority to decide. Identifying who the ultimate decision-makers are and involving them appropriately ensures your negotiation efforts are directed toward those who matter most.

Another effective tactic is finding common ground. While cultural differences are prevalent, finding shared values, goals or mutual interests can create a bridge between the parties. These commonalities can serve as a foundation on which to build agreements and foster cooperative problem-solving. Highlighting shared benefits can shift the focus from contentious points to areas of mutual gain.

The art of concession-making is also crucial in global negotiations. Different cultures have distinct approaches to giving and receiving concessions. In some cultures, the initial offer might be intentionally exaggerated, expecting a series of counteroffers and concessions. Others might present an offer closer to their final position from the outset. Understanding these tendencies helps tailor your negotiation strategy to ensure effective and reciprocated concessions.

Ethnocentrism—the tendency to view one's own culture as superior—can be a significant hindrance in cross-cultural negotiations. Cultivating an open-minded attitude and being willing to learn from the other party's perspective goes a long way. Displaying respect for their customs and traditions can foster goodwill and enhance collaboration.

Flexibility in communication styles also cannot be overlooked. Some cultures prefer high-context communication, where messages are often implicit and rely heavily on non-verbal cues. Others favor low-context communication, where the message is straightforward and explicit. Being attuned to these preferences allows you to communicate more effectively and avoid misunderstandings.

Preparation for global negotiations also includes formulating a clear negotiation agenda. By setting expectations upfront and possibly sharing the agenda with the other party beforehand, you can minimize surprises and ensure a smooth flow of discussions. This approach demonstrates transparency and helps align the focus of both parties.

Finally, the importance of post-negotiation follow-up cannot be over-stressed. In many cultures, maintaining the relationship post-negotiation is as crucial as the negotiation itself. Timely and respectful follow-up communications, delivering on promises, and continued engagement signify respect and reliability, thereby sustaining long-term partnerships.

With these strategies, you can navigate the complex landscape of global negotiations, transforming cultural diversity from a challenge into a unique advantage. By investing in cultural intelligence and honing these skills, you'll not only close deals but also build lasting, meaningful relationships across borders. This journey through global negotiations is an expedition of continuous learning and adaptability, revealing the immense potential inherent in diverse perspectives and approaches.

Understanding Ethnocentrism

In any negotiation, especially across cultures, understanding ethnocentrism is crucial for success. Ethnocentrism, the belief in the inherent superiority of one's own ethnic group or culture, can act as both a barrier and an opportunity. When not managed properly, it fosters miscommunication, biases, and misunderstandings that derail negotiations. But with awareness and proactive strategies, ethnocentrism can also be the key to unlocking deeper connections and innovative solutions.

Ethnocentrism isn't always overt. Sometimes, it's buried deep within our subconscious, influencing our judgments and actions without us even realizing it. Imagine you're in a negotiation with a team from another country. You might unconsciously judge their approach as "unprofessional" or "inefficient" simply because it's different from what you're used to. Recognizing these automatic responses is the first step in mitigating their negative effects.

Understanding the roots of ethnocentrism can help navigate its complexities. People are often naturally inclined to favor their own cultural norms because it provides a sense of comfort and security. This bias can become apparent during negotiations when unfamiliar behaviors trigger discomfort or mistrust. Knowing this can help you remain objective and open-minded in culturally diverse settings.

There are several strategies to navigate ethnocentrism in cross-cultural negotiations. One of the most effective is increasing cultural awareness and competence. This doesn't mean merely knowing a few facts about another culture but truly understanding its nuances, values, and communication styles.

Engage in research, talk to cultural experts, or even take the time to immerse yourself in different cultural experiences. This kind of deep understanding is invaluable when you're across the negotiation table.

Building strong rapport is another effective tactic. When both parties feel respected and understood, they are more likely to lower their ethnocentric defenses. Use active listening to show genuine interest in the other party's perspective. Simple gestures like learning a few phrases in their language or asking meaningful questions about their customs can go a long way in bridging cultural divides.

Let's delve into a common scenario. Imagine you're a U.S. business professional negotiating a deal with a Japanese company. The Japanese have a high-context communication style, relying heavily on non-verbal cues and the context in which something is said. On the other hand, the U.S. has a low-context communication style, where clarity and directness are valued. If you're not mindful, ethnocentrism can lead to misunderstandings and perceived disrespect. But with cultural awareness, you can adjust your communication style to align better with theirs, fostering an atmosphere of mutual respect.

Ethnocentrism doesn't just impact how we view others; it also affects how we see ourselves. A heightened sense of ethnocentrism can make us overly protective of our own ideas and less receptive to alternative viewpoints. This rigidity can be a significant obstacle in negotiations that require flexibility and creative problem-solving. Striving for self-awareness helps in recognizing when our own biases might be clouding judgment and hindering effective negotiation.

Remember that embracing cultural diversity can foster innovation. Different perspectives can lead to more comprehensive solutions and uncover new opportunities that might otherwise be overlooked. Striving to transform the initial cultural friction into a learning experience enables you to not only achieve your negotiation goals but exceed them.

There's also the role of trust. Trust is a cornerstone of any negotiation, but it's especially important in cross-cultural contexts where ethnocentrism might be lurking. Establish trust by showing consistency and integrity in your actions. Demonstrate that you value the relationship over just making a quick deal. When trust is established, it significantly reduces the influence of ethnocentric biases.

We can turn to numerous real-world examples to see the effects of un-mitigated ethnocentrism. In several high-profile business negotiations, ethnocentrism has led to disastrous outcomes simply because parties couldn't see beyond their own cultural frameworks. Conversely, companies that invest in cultural competence training often outperform those that don't, as they can better navigate the complex web of global business relations.

Practically speaking, what steps can you take to minimize the impact of ethnocentrism in your negotiations? Start by conducting a thorough cultural assessment as part of your preparation. Identify potential cultural pitfalls and plan how to address them. During the negotiation, periodically take a step back to evaluate whether ethnocentric biases are creeping into the conversation.

Another practical approach is to engage in role-playing exercises with your team, simulating cross-cultural negotiation scenarios. These exercises help in uncovering hidden biases and provide a safe space to develop strategies to counteract them. By enhancing empathy and reducing ethnocentric biases, teams can enter negotiations with a more balanced and adaptable mindset.

Consider the importance of flexibility in your negotiation strategy. Being rigidly attached to your own cultural norms can be detrimental. Instead, adopt a more fluid approach that considers the cultural context of all parties involved. This adaptability doesn't mean compromising on your core goals, but rather being open to alternative paths to achieving them.

Reflect on the importance of humility in cross-cultural negotiations. No matter how experienced you are, there's always more to learn about other cultures. Approach each negotiation with a mindset of curiosity and respect. This humility will not only endear you to your counterparts but will also enrich your own understanding and abilities.

Finally, focus on creating a culturally inclusive atmosphere during ne-gotiations. Encourage all parties to share their cultural perspectives and experiences. By fostering an environment where cultural diversity is seen as an asset rather than a hindrance, you can elevate the negotiation process and outcomes.

Understanding ethnocentrism and its impact on cross-cultural negotiations is critical for any business professional aiming to succeed in a globalized world. It requires a mindful acknowledgment of inherent biases, continuous learning, and adopting strategies that foster mutual respect and understanding. When executed well, it transforms potential barriers into stepping stones, paving the way for more meaningful and successful negotiations.

Chapter 9: The Influence of Technology

As we delve into the impact of technology on negotiation, it becomes clear that the very fabric of how deals are brokered is undergoing a radical transformation. Virtual platforms and online communication tools have revolutionized the landscape, breaking down geographical barriers and making remote negotiations not just possible but often necessary. Meanwhile, social media can extend or bolster one's influence, allowing savvy negotiators to gather intelligence and shape public perception in real-time. It's also crucial to remain vigilant about cybersecurity threats; securing sensitive information has never been more critical. While the fundamental principles of negotiation remain unchanged, technology provides new avenues and challenges, demanding a blend of timeless techniques and modern strategies to succeed. This fusion of the old and new offers a dynamic playground, where mastering the art of negotiation means embracing innovation while respecting tradition.

Online and Virtual Negotiations

We live in a digital age where technology is reshaping the landscape of business. Negotiations are no longer confined to boardrooms or face-to-face meetings.

Online and virtual negotiations have emerged as essential components of the modern business environment. Whether you're a seasoned professional or just starting in your career, understanding how to effectively negotiate in these digital spaces is crucial.

Virtual platforms offer several advantages, from convenience to cost savings.

No longer restricted by geography, you can negotiate with partners across the globe in real-time. However, virtual negotiations come with their own set of challenges that require unique strategies and skills.

The key to successful virtual negotiations rests heavily on preparation and adaptability. Unlike traditional settings, you have to adjust to a lack of physical presence and rely on different cues for communication. You must be adept at reading between the lines of written text and interpreting tone from voice alone.

First and foremost, choose the right platform. There are countless tools available—Zoom, Skype, Microsoft Teams, and more. Each has its features, but the critical aspect is choosing a reliable and user-friendly one that all parties are comfortable with.

Technical issues can quickly derail a negotiation. Ensure your connection is stable, your microphone and camera are functioning well, and the software is updated. It's a good idea to conduct a test run before the actual negotiation to iron out any technical hiccups.

In a virtual setting, facial expressions and body language are often limited to what's visible on a screen. This can make it challenging to gauge the other party's reactions. Being expressive with your face and gestures can help bridge this gap. Smile genuinely, nod to show understanding, and maintain eye contact with the camera to simulate face-to-face conversation.

Non-verbal communication still plays a significant role, even through a screen. Be mindful of your posture and screen presence; slouching or appearing distracted can give off the wrong impression. Position yourself in a well-lit area with a neutral background to minimize distractions.

When it comes to the actual negotiation, clarity is paramount. Misunder-standings are easier to occur without the cues of a physical presence. Speak clearly, use simple language, and regularly summarize points discussed to ensure all parties are on the same page.

Building rapport in a virtual setting requires extra effort. Start with small talk to create a more comfortable atmosphere, just as you would in person. Share something relatable to build a connection. Personal touches can go a long way in establishing trust, even in a digital format.

Utilize the chat functions of your chosen platform to complement verbal communication. Sending links to relevant documents or sharing screens can enhance clarity and support your points. These features can be powerful tools when used correctly.

Avoid multitasking during a virtual negotiation. Resist the temptation to check emails or browse other tabs. The other party can often sense divided attention, which can be detrimental to building trust. Focus entirely on the negotiation, just as you would in a face-to-face meeting.

Prepare to handle silence effectively. Virtual communications often have slight delays, so what might feel like an uncomfortable pause can merely be a lag in transmission. Give the other party space to speak, and don't rush to fill every moment of silence. Sometimes, a brief pause can lead to valuable insights or concessions.

Emotional intelligence is just as crucial in virtual negotiations as in traditional settings. Be empathetic and attentive to the subtle emotions that may arise. Acknowledge any signs of frustration or misunderstanding and address them promptly.

Remember, the digital world retains records. Every chat message, email, and document shared can be logged. Be mindful of this permanence and conduct yourself with the same professionalism and ethics you would in any other context.

Another unique aspect of online negotiations is the possibility of asynchronous communication. Time zones differences can sometimes necessitate this approach. When negotiating via email or other non-live platforms, be especially clear, concise, and thorough in your communications, leaving little room for misinterpretation.

When negotiating over multiple sessions, continuity is key. Keep detailed notes and summarize past discussions at the beginning of each meeting to ensure a consistent progression. This ensures no critical points are overlooked or forgotten in the digital shuffle.

The virtual setting can also benefit from the inclusion of visual aids. Infographics, charts, and slides can bolster your arguments and provide visual clarity. These can be effortlessly shared via screen-sharing functions, making your negotiation more compelling.

Don't underestimate the power of follow-up in virtual negotiations. After each session, send concise summaries of what was discussed and agreed upon. This not only reinforces the terms but also reduces the risk of misunderstandings.

Virtual negotiations require a blend of traditional negotiation skills and new, tech-savvy strategies. Adaptability is your greatest asset. Embrace the convenience and global reach that technology offers while remaining aware of its limitations.

The landscape may have shifted, but the essence of negotiation remains— it's about creating value, understanding needs, and building relationships. Mastering online and virtual negotiations means you can harness technology's benefits to achieve your goals, no matter where in the world you find yourself.

The Role of Social Media

In today's digital age, social media stands as one of the most influential tools in the realm of negotiation. The rise of platforms like LinkedIn, Facebook, Twitter, and Instagram has fundamentally changed how we communicate, gather information, and influence others. These changes reverberate through every aspect of business negotiations.

Social media serves as a powerful catalyst for building one's personal brand. Your online presence can shape how potential negotiation partners perceive you long before any in-person meeting. Curating a professional profile, sharing insightful content, and actively engaging with industry leaders can establish credibility and trust, which are foundational to effective negotiation.

The transparency offered by social media can be a double-edged sword. On one hand, a public profile can bolster your reputation. On the other hand, it exposes you to scrutiny. People can easily look up your background, past comments, and engagement history, which might be leveraged against you during negotiations. Thus, maintaining a consistent and professional presence online is paramount.

Imagine walking into a negotiation room already knowing your counterpart's preferences, interests, and even pain points. Social media platforms offer a wealth of information that can be utilized for this exact purpose. With a few clicks, you can gather insights into the other party's company culture, recent achievements, and ongoing challenges. Such knowledge positions you as a well-informed negotiator who can tailor proposals to address the specific needs and interests of the other party.

Influence and persuasion are two critical elements of negotiation, and social media amplifies your capacity to wield these tools. By sharing valuable content and participating in meaningful conversations, you create a narrative that positions you as an authority in your field. This perception can significantly affect the negotiating dynamics, giving you a psychological edge even before discussions begin.

Moreover, social media enables real-time updates and communication. Announcements about new products, partnerships, or organizational changes can all be instantly disseminated to a global audience. Staying attuned to these updates can offer crucial timing advantages in negotiations. For instance, knowing about a recent merger just announced on their company's LinkedIn page can help you better frame your offer during a business negotiation.

It's also essential to recognize the role of social listening. By monitoring mentions of your own brand and that of your counterparts, you can gauge sentiment and anticipate challenges or opportunities. Tools for social listening can analyze trends and conversations, giving you insights into stakeholder concerns, competitive positioning, and potential leverage points.

Let's not underestimate the importance of digital networking. Platforms like LinkedIn provide unparalleled opportunities to connect with industry professionals, investors, and potential clients. Building a robust network before entering any negotiation can yield support and references that may tip the scales in your favor. Reaching out to mutual connections for introductions or recommendations can add a layer of trust and validation to your interactions.

However, it's crucial to navigate the perils of misinformation and perception management. Social media can rapidly spread false information, which could potentially damage your reputation or that of the organization you represent. Inaccurate or negative portrayals can severely undermine your negotiating position. Being vigilant about the authenticity and accuracy of your posts and engagements is critical.

Engaging in discussions, replying to comments, and acknowledging compliments or addressing complaints shows transparency and builds relationships. This not only improves your public image but also showcases your willingness to engage and communicate openly, a trait highly valued in negotiations.

Additionally, it's wise to consider how social media can be used to manage crises or setbacks in negotiations. Rapid dissemination of a well-crafted, transparent message can help control the narrative and mitigate damage. Promptly addressing any misunderstandings or disputes through public or private messages can also showcase conflict resolution skills and a proactive attitude.

As technology continues to advance, social media will evolve, bringing new challenges and opportunities for negotiators. Keeping abreast of these developments and understanding how to leverage them effectively will be crucial. Embrace these tools as part of your strategic arsenal. As you harness the power of social media, let it inspire you to be more insightful, connected, and influential.

Ultimately, the merging of social media with traditional negotiation techniques can create a more dynamic and informed approach. Embrace the potential it offers while remaining wary of its complexities. By strategically managing your social media presence and engaging with your network, you can navigate the negotiation landscape with greater confidence and skill.

Cybersecurity Concerns

As technology continues to permeate various aspects of our lives, its influence on negotiation processes can't be understated. However, along with the vast benefits, technology also brings significant cybersecurity concerns that business professionals must be aware of. Information is power in negotiation, and in the digital age, protecting that information is paramount. One cybersecurity breach can unravel months of meticulous planning and preparation, leaving negotiators at a substantial disadvantage.

Imagine you've entered into a high-stakes negotiation with thorough research and strategically set objectives. Now, imagine all that information—your strengths, weaknesses, and planned tactics—falling into the hands of the opposing party due to a cybersecurity breach. The ramifications could be disastrous. This scenario underscores why cybersecurity should be a cornerstone of modern negotiation strategies. Securing sensitive data isn't just an IT department's responsibility anymore; it's a critical aspect of a negotiator's toolbox.

Let's delve into how cybersecurity concerns can affect various stages of negotiation. During the preparation stage, negotiators compile reams of sensitive data, often stored digitally. These digital storage solutions—from cloud services to internal servers—are prime targets for hackers. It's crucial to recognize that a comprehensive cybersecurity strategy should involve both technological defenses and team training.

For instance, using advanced encryption methods and secure communication channels can protect conversations and data from prying eyes. Access controls should be meticulously managed, restricting sensitive information to only those who absolutely need it. Remember, even the most advanced technological defenses can be undermined by human error. Training your team on cybersecurity best practices can make them the first line of defense against potential breaches.

Virtual negotiations, now more common than ever, present their own set of cybersecurity challenges. Video conferencing platforms, while convenient, are not immune to hacking. Unauthorized access to virtual meetings can lead to information leaks and strategic disadvantages. Before starting any virtual negotiation, ensure that the platform is secure. Utilize password protections, monitor for unwelcome participants, and prefer platforms known for robust security measures.

Social media is another area where cybersecurity meets negotiation. The wealth of information available through social media can be a double-edged sword. While it offers valuable insights into your counterpart's behavior and preferences, it also presents a vulnerability. One careless tweet or LinkedIn post could give away more than intended, providing competitors with critical knowledge about your negotiation stance. Be cautious about what's shared online, and educate your team on the potential risks.

Another crucial aspect is the legal implications associated with cybersecurity lapses. Breaches can lead to severe legal consequences, including financial penalties and damaged reputations. For instance, if a breach results in the exposure of confidential client data, you could face not only client loss but also possible lawsuits. Thus, understanding the regulations and ensuring compliance is essential.

Additionally, think about the loss of credibility that inevitably follows a data breach. Trust is fundamental in negotiation, and any indication that your data handling practices are lax could erode that trust rapidly. Even your closest business allies might start questioning the safety of their data in your hands. Hence, cybersecurity should be seen as a trust-building measure as much as a protective one.

Incorporating comprehensive cybersecurity measures into your negotiation strategy is no longer optional; it's necessary. But where do you start? First, conduct a thorough risk assessment of your current digital infrastructure. Identify the weakest links and potential points of entry for cyber threats. This assessment will guide the implementation of effective cybersecurity controls.

Next, consider employing zero-trust architecture, a security model that operates under the assumption that every attempt to access information is a potential threat. This model enforces strict verification processes, ensuring that only authorized personnel can access sensitive data. This proactive approach significantly enhances your security posture.

Furthermore, stay updated with current cybersecurity trends and threats. Cybercriminals are continually evolving their tactics, and staying a step ahead requires constant vigilance. Regular training sessions and updates are essential to keep your team informed about the latest threats and how to counter them.

In high-stakes negotiations, the adoption of digital ledger technologies like blockchain can offer unrivaled security. Blockchain's decentralized nature makes it highly resistant to tampering. Implementing such technologies could provide an additional layer of security, especially in negotiations involving significant transactions or sensitive data.

Moreover, don't overlook the importance of having a robust incident response plan. Despite your best efforts, breaches can still happen. How you respond can determine the extent of the damage. An effective incident response plan should include immediate actions to contain the breach, communication strategies to inform stakeholders, and steps for recovery and mitigation.

While technology continues to shape the landscape of negotiation, recognizing and addressing cybersecurity concerns is crucial. By integrating advanced security measures, fostering a culture of vigilance, and staying informed about evolving threats, you can safeguard your negotiation processes. This proactive approach not only protects your valuable data but also enhances your credibility and trustworthiness in the negotiating arena.

In conclusion, cybersecurity isn't merely a technical concern; it's a strategic imperative. As business professionals and negotiators, it's incumbent upon us to protect the integrity of our negotiation processes. By doing so, we not only shield ourselves from potential threats but also build a foundation of trust and reliability that is essential for successful negotiations. The digital age demands a new caliber of preparedness—align your strategies with robust cybersecurity practices and transform challenges into opportunities for securing the best possible outcomes.

Chapter 10: Ethical Considerations

As we dive into the crux of ethical considerations, let's remind ourselves that negotiation isn't just a dance of strategies and tactics—it's a human endeavor grounded in trust and integrity. Establishing clear ethical boundaries not only fortifies your reputation but also builds long-lasting relationships. Imagine the ripple effect of one decision: ethical lapses may yield short-term gains, but they can erode your credibility and, ultimately, your career. The stories of fallen giants in the business world serve as poignant reminders of the consequences of unethical behavior. Balancing ambition with an unwavering commitment to ethical principles transforms negotiations from mere transactions to powerful opportunities for mutual growth. As you operate within this dynamic landscape, let your compass always point towards fairness and transparency, ensuring that every deal you seal contributes to a legacy of trust and respect.

Establishing Ethical Boundaries

Ethical boundaries are the invisible lines we draw to maintain integrity, fairness, and respect in our negotiations. They aren't just rules, they're principles that guide our actions and decisions. In a world where the line between right and wrong can often blur, establishing these boundaries ahead of time can be your moral compass.

The first step in establishing ethical boundaries is self-awareness. Understand your values and principles. What matters most to you? Is it honesty, transparency, or perhaps fairness? Knowing your core values will help you make decisions that align with your ethical standards. This self-awareness is not just important for personal satisfaction; it also contributes to long-term success. Establishing a reputation as someone who can be trusted goes a long way in building lasting business relationships.

Once you've defined your values, it's crucial to communicate them clearly to others. Make it known what your ethical boundaries are from the get-go. For instance, you might say, "I believe in being honest about what we can achieve together." This transparency helps in setting the tone for negotiations and clarifies expectations. Silence in this regard can often be mistaken for consent, leading to situations where ethical boundaries are crossed without your approval.

Setting these boundaries doesn't mean you have to be rigid. Flexibility within ethical constraints is essential for effective negotiation. The key here is to distinguish between being flexible in your tactics and compromising your ethical standards. While you might adjust your negotiation strategies, such as offering concessions or recalibrating your approach based on new information, your core principles should remain non-negotiable. This structured flexibility allows you to navigate complex situations without compromising on what truly matters.

However, even with well-defined ethical boundaries, you'll inevitably face ethical dilemmas. The pressure to succeed, the desire to close a deal, or the influence of less scrupulous counterparts can all test your limits. During these times, it's crucial to stay anchored to your ethical framework. Reflect on past experiences where you've faced similar dilemmas. What did you learn from those situations? Incorporate those lessons into your current decision-making process.

Another key aspect is to seek input from trusted colleagues or mentors. Sometimes, a fresh perspective can offer solutions that align with your ethical boundaries while still achieving your objectives. Utilize these resources effectively, and don't hesitate to take a step back if you feel you're being pushed to compromise your ethics. It's better to temporarily halt negotiations than to proceed down a path you'll later regret.

Moreover, consider the long-term implications of crossing ethical boundaries. Sure, a quick win might seem appealing, but unethical behavior can have far-reaching consequences. Loss of credibility, damaged relationships, and even legal repercussions can follow. The business world is tightly knit; word travels fast. Being known as someone who upholds strong ethical principles will serve you well, earning you respect and loyalty from clients and peers alike.

Evaluating the moral compass of the organizations or parties you're negotiating with is also essential. Just as you have ethical boundaries, so do others. Ensure there's congruence. If the party you're dealing with has a history of unethical behavior, proceed with caution. Despite the potential for immediate gains, the risks involved in partnering with such entities often outweigh the benefits.

Know that ethical boundaries aren't static; they evolve based on experiences and changing societal norms. Hence, it's important to periodically reassess and adjust them. Continuous learning and self-reflection can help you stay aligned with your core values while adapting to new challenges.

To reinforce your ethical mindset, consider creating a code of conduct for your negotiation practices. This document could outline your ethical boundaries and serve as a reference point for both you and your team. Incorporate elements like honesty, fairness, confidentiality, and mutual respect into this code. It's not just a formality; it's a commitment to uphold a standard that fosters trust and integrity in all your dealings.

Establishing ethical boundaries also involves recognizing and mitigating conflicts of interest. Conflicts of interest can skew your judgment, leading you to make decisions that are not in the best interest of all parties. Be transparent about any potential conflicts from the outset and take steps to address them proactively. This transparency builds trust and prevents future misunderstandings.

You might find yourself in situations where both parties have conflicting ethical standards. In such cases, focus on finding common ground. Engage in open and honest dialogue to understand each other's viewpoints and work towards a solution that respects both parties' boundaries. This collaborative approach often leads to more sustainable and satisfying outcomes for everyone involved.

Lastly, remember that ethical boundaries are not just about avoiding misconduct but actively pursuing ethical excellence. Strive to exceed the minimum standards and become a role model in ethical negotiations. Your commitment to ethics won't just benefit you; it will elevate the standard of conduct within your professional community. Inspire others through your actions, showing that ethical boundaries are not obstacles but pathways to true and lasting success.

By adhering to these principles, you not only protect your integrity but also create a positive ripple effect in your professional endeavors. Ethical boundaries, once firmly established, serve as both a shield and a beacon, guiding you through the complex and often murky waters of negotiation.

This commitment to ethics might seem daunting at times, especially when faced with high-stakes situations, but it is precisely during these moments that adherence to one's ethical boundaries becomes paramount. Hold the line. In the grand scheme of things, being ethical will invariably lead to greater respect, stronger relationships, and more meaningful success.

Consequences of Unethical Behavior

Unethical behavior in negotiations can lead to a cascade of negative reper-cussions, both immediate and long-term. While the allure of short-term gains may be tempting, the eventual costs often far outweigh these benefits. Business professionals need to understand that integrity isn't just a buzzword; it's a cornerstone of sustainable success.

Let's first consider the immediate impacts. If you're caught engaging in deceptive tactics, the fallout can be severe. Trust, which is painstakingly built, can be shattered in an instant. The other party will question every previous and future interaction, undermining your credibility and damaging your reputation. Without trust, even the most meticulously crafted negotiation strategy can crumble, leaving you with less than what you aimed for.

In professional circles, news about unethical behavior spreads quickly. Imagine being blacklisted or finding yourself the subject of cautionary whispers in industry meetings and networking events. Your future negotiation opportunities could evaporate, replaced by the growing reluctance of others to engage with someone who's gained a reputation for deceit. This damage to your professional network can severely limit future career prospects and business opportunities.

Financial consequences also loom large. Think of lawsuits, penalties, and the potential loss of lucrative contracts. Companies cannot afford to have their reputation tarnished by the unethical actions of their representatives. This loss of trust often results in decreased business, higher scrutiny from regulators, and the potential collapse of long-term partnerships. When major clients or partners walk away, it can mean significant revenue loss, sometimes even threatening the very survival of the business.

Moreover, unethical behavior can erode team morale. Your colleagues and subordinates watch closely, and when they see unethical tactics being rewarded or ignored, it complicates the ethical landscape of the organization. There's not just a risk of them emulating bad behavior; it can also lead to a toxic work environment where accountability and integrity are devalued. Over time, this can drive away high-caliber talent who seek workplaces aligned with their personal values.

Legal ramifications can't be overlooked either. Engaging in unethical practices increases the risk of ending up entangled in legal battles. Fraudulent misrepresentation, for example, can expose you to lawsuits that could be both financially draining and damaging to your public image. These legal issues can persist for years, draining resources and sapping organizational energy that could be better spent on growth and innovation.

The personal toll of unethical conduct also deserves attention. Living under the constant stress of potential exposure can be mentally and emotionally exhausting. It affects your well-being and can take a toll on your personal relationships. Over time, the psychological burden of knowing you've compromised your integrity can lead to burnout, dissatisfaction, and even depression.

On a broader scale, consider the societal impact. Ethical behavior in negotiations helps maintain the market's integrity. When unethical practices become commonplace, it erodes public trust in industries and institutions, leading to a cynical, mistrustful environment that stifles innovation and collaboration. Remember, as business professionals, we have a role to play in upholding the standards of our industries.

Interestingly, ethical behavior in negotiation also serves to elevate the profession. Imagine being known as a negotiator who is assertive yet fair, ambitious yet trustworthy. These qualities not only distinguish you but also elevate the negotiation profession itself. The prestige and respect accorded to such professionalism can open doors you never anticipated.

Challenges will come your way, tests of your ethical boundaries will arise, but staying committed to ethical principles ensures you play the long game. And the long game, as seasoned negotiators will tell you, is where true success lies. Ethical conduct builds a magnetic reputation, attracts invaluable alliances, and creates opportunities for genuine, lasting success.

Finally, let's remember that business isn't just about the next deal; it's about building something enduring. Long-term success and impact stem from relationships grounded in trust and mutual respect. Ethical behavior may not always provide immediate gratification, but it lays the foundation for a career and business that can withstand the test of time.

Case Studies in Ethical Dilemmas

Sometimes, negotiations aren't just about who gets the best deal—they're about what's right and what's wrong. Ethical dilemmas in negotiation force us to confront our principles and question the integrity of our actions. They challenge us to balance competitive instincts with moral considerations, testing the boundaries of what we are willing to compromise.

Take the case of a pharmaceutical company negotiating drug prices with a developing country. The stakes are incredibly high: the cost of medication could determine whether millions of people have access to life-saving treatments. The company has invested heavily in research and development and has shareholders to answer to, but the ethical implications of setting exorbitant prices can't be ignored. This complex negotiation goes beyond profits and losses, delving into issues of social responsibility and moral duty.

In another scenario, consider a tech startup grappling with an ethical quandary in its negotiations with a major social media company. The startup has developed an algorithm that could significantly enhance user engagement. However, internal tests have shown that this algorithm may contribute to social divisiveness by promoting polarizing content. The startup's founders are faced with a daunting ethical dilemma: Should they proceed with a lucrative deal that could propel their business forward, despite potential negative social impacts?

Ethical dilemmas can also arise within the confines of an organization, compelling employees and leaders to navigate murky waters. Picture a mid-level manager who discovers that her company is negotiating a deal with a supplier known for unethical labor practices. Her dilemma is personal and professional: doing nothing compromises her morals, but blowing the whistle could jeopardize her career and financial stability.

These ethical puzzles often don't have clear-cut answers, which is why they are so challenging. They require negotiators to consider not only the immediate outcomes but also the long-term impact on their own integrity and the broader society. Parties must weigh the benefits of gaining an advantage against the moral cost, making decisions that align with their ethical compasses.

Consider the controversy surrounding clothing retailers and their supply chains. Reports emerged that factories using child labor and unsafe working conditions were providing apparel for well-known brands. Retailers faced a moral imperative during negotiations with suppliers: either demand better labor practices, likely resulting in higher costs, or ignore these practices to maintain lower prices.

Corporations today operate under the scrutiny of a vigilant public, making ethical considerations even more critical. Social media amplifies any misstep, potentially causing irreversible damage to a company's reputation. An exemplary case involves the fast-food giant negotiating sourcing contracts. With growing awareness about animal welfare and environmental sustainability, the company had to decide whether to adopt more humane and eco-friendly practices at the risk of increased expenses. This delicate balance between profit and ethics highlighted the need for conscientious decision-making.

The field of bioengineering offers another stark illustration. Innovators in genetic modification face ethical dilemmas regarding human enhancement and agricultural biotech. Negotiations for funding and implementation frequently bring up ethical concerns. For instance, genetically modified organisms (GMOs) may significantly boost food production, but they also raise questions about long-term environmental effects and the ethics of altering natural species. Stakeholders in these negotiations must grapple with potential benefits against ethical and ecological risks.

Now, let's look at the financial sector—a realm where ethics often collide with ruthless competition. The 2008 financial crisis unveiled numerous ethical lapses among financial institutions. Before the meltdown, many firms engaged in negotiations over complex financial products without full disclosure of risks, leading to catastrophic consequences. These unethical practices eroded trust and resulted in a global economic downturn, underscoring the dire need for ethical vigilance in finance.

Education sectors aren't immune to ethical dilemmas either. University administrators frequently face tough negotiations over partnership deals and research funding. The question often hinges on whether to accept funds from corporations with questionable ethics. Such decisions can impact the institution's reputation and the future of its research endeavors. Maintaining ethical standards in these negotiations is a testament to a university's integrity and its commitment to societal well-being.

Public sector negotiations also come under the ethical spotlight. Government officials often negotiate contracts for public projects, where transparency, fairness, and the public good should take precedence. Corruption and favoritism can undermine these negotiations, leading to imbalanced outcomes that favor a few while disadvantaging many. Ethical considerations here are not just a matter of policy but of public trust and governance.

When negotiating across cultures, ethical dilemmas compound further with varying ethical standards and practices. What is deemed acceptable in one culture might be considered unethical in another. This can pose a significant challenge for international negotiators who must navigate these waters carefully, aligning their actions with both local customs and global ethical standards. Respect for diversity and ethical consistency become paramount.

Ethics in negotiation also resonate on a personal level. Day-to-day business interactions are peppered with smaller ethical decisions. For example, during salary negotiations, both employers and employees might face an ethical tug-of-war between fair compensation and budget constraints. These micro-level ethical decisions are just as impactful on a personal and organizational level as the high-stakes cases mentioned earlier.

As these case studies demonstrate, ethical dilemmas demand a multi-dimensional perspective, incorporating empathy, foresight, and unwavering integrity. They remind us that our decisions in negotiations ripple outwards, affecting not just the immediate parties but society at large. Embracing such an ethical outlook transforms negotiators from mere deal-makers into stewards of trust and integrity.

Navigating these ethical dilemmas involves more than just adhering to rules; it encompasses a profound understanding of the moral landscape in which we operate. A thorough grasp of ethical principles coupled with inspired commitment to them is crucial. Every negotiation becomes an opportunity to reinforce ethical standards, demonstrating that achieving success need not come at the cost of integrity.

In conclusion, ethical dilemmas in negotiation aren't just obstacles— they're opportunities for growth and reflection. By striving for ethical excellence, we not only elevate our negotiation skills but also contribute positively to our industries and communities. Ethical negotiation isn't merely about reaching an agreement; it's about achieving the right kind of success.

Chapter 11: Negotiating in Personal Life

N egotiation isn't just a business tool; it's a life skill that becomes incredibly valuable in personal settings. Imagine the daily interactions with family, friends, and even with yourself as a series of negotiations. From planning a family vacation to deciding on household chores, each discussion has the potential to strengthen relationships or create tensions. By employing strategies like active listening and empathetic understanding, you can transform conflicts into opportunities for deeper connection. Whether you're mediating a sibling squabble or convincing a friend to try a new restaurant, approaching these interactions with the same preparation and creativity used in professional negotiations can yield surprisingly fruitful results. Recognize that compromises in the personal sphere don't signify loss but rather mutual respect and growth, setting a foundation for a more harmonious life. This chapter explores the nuanced dynamics of negotiating within the comfort of our personal lives, emphasizing the importance of patience, honesty, and a touch of humor to navigate the complexities of human relationships effectively.

Family and Relationship Negotiations

Navigating the labyrinth of family and relationship negotiations can be one of life's most intricate yet most rewarding challenges. Unlike business settings, where the stakes are often measured in fiscal terms, family negotiations are deeply emotional, affecting our closest relationships. It's crucial to understand that successful negotiation within the family doesn't mean outmaneuvering the other person. Instead, it involves harmonizing differences to find mutually beneficial outcomes. Family negotiations are less about winning and more about finding common ground, nurturing relationships, and maintaining emotional health.

First, let's address an important yet often overlooked aspect: empathy. Empathy in family negotiations can be a transformative force. When you genuinely endeavor to understand the other person's perspective, you can preempt a lot of misunderstandings and conflicts. Empathy is a two-way street; it cannot be one-sided. Balancing your needs with the needs of others is essential. This can only happen when everyone involved feels heard and understood. Establishing this emotional connection can pave the way for more open and fruitful discussions.

Consider non-verbal communication—a dimension often overshadowed by the words we speak. Family settings are breeding grounds for non-verbal cues. A frown, a sigh, or even crossed arms can be loaded with meaning. Pay attention to these cues just as you would in a boardroom. They often reveal hidden concerns that need addressing. A conscious effort to maintain open body language, such as eye contact and welcoming gestures, can rapidly build trust and comfort.

In the realm of tactics, understanding the subtleties between a competitive and a collaborative approach is key. Unlike business negotiations where competitiveness might be more accepted, a more collaborative approach generally yields better results in family settings. Imagine negotiating with your spouse about the division of household responsibilities. Approaching the conversation with a win-lose mentality can strain your relationship. Instead, try a collaborative approach where both parties feel like they have gained something. This approach will fortify not just the immediate outcome but the long-term relationship as well.

Setting objectives and priorities is as pertinent in family negotiations as it is in business. What are the must-haves in this discussion for you, and what can you compromise on? These priorities could range from financial decisions to lifestyle choices. For example, deciding on holiday plans requires a clear understanding of each other's priorities. Is spending time with extended family more important, or is a restful holiday just for the immediate family the priority? Knowing what's non-negotiable can simplify the conversation and avoid unnecessary friction.

Let's also talk about managing conflict and tension—a frequent visitor in family discussions. Conflicts can escalate quickly in familial settings due to the emotional ties involved. Addressing the issue when tempers are high is often counterproductive. Taking a moment to cool down and regroup can offer immense benefits. This "cooling-off" period allows for more rational and thoughtful discussions. Remember, the goal is not just to resolve the conflict but to maintain a healthy relationship.

The principles of BATNA (Best Alternative To a Negotiated Agreement) and ZOPA (Zone of Possible Agreement) aren't just for the boardroom; they're equally relevant at home. Understanding your best alternative if a particular negotiation falls through can provide clarity. For instance, if you're negotiating a family budget and can't reach an agreement, knowing your alternative options can prevent prolonged stalemates and bring the discussion back to a more productive path. The concept of ZOPA can help identify areas where mutual agreement is possible, turning potential conflicts into opportunities for collaboration.

One especially complex family negotiation is that involving children. Balancing parental authority while giving children a voice can be a tightrope walk. Negotiations with children should be guided by a mix of firmness and understanding. For example, a discussion about screen time can evolve from a dreaded conflict into a constructive dialogue when parents validate children's feelings and explain their concerns clearly. Giving children some control, within boundaries, can make them more likely to respect the agreed-upon rules.

Emotions often run high in family settings, so it's essential to manage not just your emotions but also to recognize and respect the emotions of others. Acknowledging emotions doesn't mean conceding to every emotional outburst, but it does mean validating the feelings behind them. Statements like "I understand you're feeling stressed about this" can diffuse tension and create a more congenial environment for negotiation.

To bring another dimension into the conversation, consider the role of extended family. In-laws, siblings, and even grandparents can have an undeniable impact. Their expectations and influences can complicate family negotiations. It's crucial to establish boundaries while considering their viewpoints. For example, when buying a new house, you might face pressure from relatives with differing opinions. Balancing these perspectives while keeping your immediate family's priorities at the forefront can be challenging but absolutely necessary.

Let's not forget about financial negotiations within the family. Whether it's budgeting, saving for college, or planning for retirement, financial decisions can be a minefield of emotions and differing priorities. Full transparency and regular check-ins can help. Establishing a family financial plan where everyone's goals are visible can reduce misunderstandings. It's not just about managing money but managing expectations and fostering a sense of unity and shared purpose.

As we delve deeper into personal negotiations, it's clear that every family dynamic is unique. What works in one family might not work in another. That's why flexibility and continuous learning are crucial. Be open to adjusting your strategies based on what resonates best with your family. The ultimate goal is to build stronger, more resilient relationships where everyone feels heard, valued, and respected.

Finally, think about the long-term impact of these negotiations. Effective family negotiations are investments in the future. They don't just solve immediate issues but lay the groundwork for better understanding and cooperation down the road. As with any skill, mastery comes with practice and reflection. After every negotiation, take a moment to reflect on what worked well and what could be improved. Continuous improvement is the key to mastering the art of family and relationship negotiations.

Whether it's dividing household chores, planning a family vacation, or making major life decisions, approaching family and relationship negotiations with empathy, strategic thinking, and a collaborative mindset can transform challenges into opportunities for growth and connection. By incorporating these principles and continuously honing your skills, you can navigate these intricate discussions with grace and efficacy, strengthening the bonds that matter most.

Negotiating for Personal Gains

Life is full of negotiations, ranging from career changes to simple disagreements at home. Often, the stakes involve our personal growth and fulfillment. Learning how to negotiate for personal gains isn't just about getting what you want; it's about improving your quality of life. It's about understanding your value, setting boundaries, and acquiring the skills to advocate for yourself in various scenarios. This is not just an external journey but an internal one as well, requiring self-awareness, confidence, and resilience.

Negotiation in the personal realm comes with its own unique challenges and opportunities. These negotiations often take place in environments laden with emotions and history, where logic and rationality might easily get clouded by feelings. In this context, the first step towards success is a strong understanding of your own needs and desires. Self-awareness empowers you to articulate clearly what you want and why you deserve it.

For instance, let's consider asking for a raise at work. It's not merely about the monetary gain; it's about seeking acknowledgment for your contributions. To do this effectively, you need to understand your strengths, gather evidence of your achievements, and frame your request in a way that aligns with the company's goals. The same principles apply whether you are discussing division of household chores or negotiating terms in a relationship.

Moreover, when negotiating for personal gains, empathy and listening skills become especially critical. To quote an experienced negotiator, "The art of negotiation lies in understanding the other party as deeply as you understand yourself." Recognize that the person across the table may have their own struggles and motivations. Acknowledging these can create a more cooperative atmosphere, turning what could be a conflict into an opportunity for mutual growth.

One powerful approach is to leverage the give-and-take method. This involves being prepared to offer concessions to the other party to achieve your own goals. For example, if you're negotiating for more personal time with your significant other, you might also offer to take up additional tasks that they find burdensome. This method fosters a sense of partnership and shared objectives rather than an adversarial stand-off.

Understanding the concept of Best Alternative to a Negotiated Agreement (BATNA) can also be invaluable in personal negotiations. BATNA is essentially your backup plan if the current negotiations fail. Knowing your alternatives provides you with leverage and reduces the fear of walking away from a bad deal. For instance, if you're negotiating a rent reduction with your landlord, your BATNA might be that you've already identified a more affordable housing option. This knowledge enhances your confidence and bargaining position.

Another key aspect is timing. In personal negotiations, picking the right moment can significantly influence the outcome. Bringing up a contentious topic during a stressful or inconvenient time can hamper the negotiation process. Instead, choose a time when all parties are calm and open to discussion. This simple but effective strategy can greatly enhance the chances of a successful negotiation.

Personal gains also extend to self-negotiation—the ongoing dialogue you have with yourself. Setting personal goals, prioritizing activities, and managing time effectively are forms of negotiation we constantly engage in. Here, establishing clear objectives and realistic expectations can be transformative. For example, if you aim to dedicate more time to a hobby, negotiate other aspects of your schedule to make room for it. Setting measurable milestones can help keep you on track.

Of course, not all personal negotiations will go smoothly. It's essential to stay patient and persistent, learning from each encounter. Reflect on what worked and what didn't, and be adaptable enough to adjust your strategies. Remember to celebrate even your small victories; these are often the stepping stones to larger, more significant achievements.

Finally, never underestimate the power of a well-prepared negotiation. Before entering any negotiation, invest time in researching and gathering all the necessary information. This preparation will allow you to present your case compellingly and convincingly. Whether it's knowing market salaries for a raise or understanding common childcare arrangements for co-parenting negotiations, informed negotiations are generally more successful.

In conclusion, negotiating for personal gains is an art that encompasses understanding one's value, setting boundaries, and fostering empathy. It's about creating a win-win scenario where both parties feel acknowledged and fulfilled. By honing your skills and strategies, you can turn everyday interactions into opportunities for personal development and enhanced quality of life. This journey requires patience, resilience, and a commitment to continual learning. However, the rewards—achieving your goals and improving your overall happiness—are well worth the effort.

Conflict Resolution at Home

Conflict at home is inevitable, but how we handle it can make all the difference between harmony and ongoing tension. Successful conflict resolution requires more than just addressing the issue at hand; it involves understanding underlying emotions, building empathy, and leveraging negotiation skills to reach amicable solutions.

Imagine a situation where you and your partner are disagreeing about household chores. You think you're doing more than your fair share, and your partner feels the same way about their contributions. It's easy for this disagreement to spiral into resentment. However, taking a step back to approach the situation like a seasoned negotiator can transform the conflict into an opportunity for strengthening your relationship.

First, acknowledge the feelings involved. Emotions are powerful drivers in any conflict. By validating your partner's feelings, you start to build a bridge of empathy. Acknowledge their perspective even before you lay out yours. This doesn't mean you agree with them, but it shows that you respect their viewpoint.

"The foundation of successful conflict resolution lies in active listening," says many communication experts. "Active listening involves fully concentrating, understanding, and responding thoughtfully." Let your partner speak without interruptions. Often, just letting someone express their frustration can significantly reduce the emotional charge of the situation, opening pathways for constructive dialogue.

When both parties have aired their grievances, it's time to identify common ground. What do you both genuinely want? Perhaps it's a cleaner home or more leisure time. With shared goals in sight, begin working towards a mutually beneficial solution. Consider each other's strengths and constraints. If one enjoys cooking, maybe they can take on that task, while the other handles cleaning.

While negotiating, aim for solutions that are equitable but not necessarily equal. Fairness doesn't always imply a 50-50 split; it means arrangements that reflect both parties' circumstances and contributions. Use "I" statements to express your feelings and needs without sounding accusatory. For example, say, "I feel overwhelmed by the cleaning and would appreciate your help," instead of, "You never help with the cleaning."

Maintaining flexibility during negotiations is crucial. If one solution doesn't work out, be willing to explore other options. Just as in business, your 'BATNA'—Best Alternative to a Negotiated Agreement—at home is your fallback plan. Knowing what you can do independently if a solution isn't reached adds a layer of confidence but use this knowledge constructively, not as a threat.

Assessing the emotional climate is vital when dealing with more significant conflicts, like parenting styles or financial decisions. Children observing their parents handle disagreements with tact and empathy can be profoundly educational and beneficial for their development. Here, emotional intelligence plays a crucial role. Recognizing and managing your emotions—and those of your partner—can diffuse tension. Sometimes, taking a break and returning to the discussion later can prevent tempers from flaring.

Remember, non-verbal cues are as vital as spoken words. Pay attention to body language, facial expressions, and tone of voice. Sometimes, a soft touch or a compassionate look can convey more understanding than a thousand words. Non-verbal communication establishes a baseline of trust and comfort, essential for negotiating delicate issues.

However, there are times when even the best negotiation strategies seem to hit a wall. It's not uncommon to face deadlocks at home just as in business. The key is to remain calm and patient. "Mutual respect and a willingness to understand the other person's perspective can dissolve even the most hardened stand-offs," say seasoned mediators. Compromise does not signify defeat but an acknowledgment that the relationship is more important than individual victory.

Invoking third-party mediation for severe, recurring conflicts isn't a sign of failure, but wisdom. Whether a therapist or a family counselor, an objective third party can offer new perspectives and tools for resolution. These professionals are skilled at identifying underlying issues that may not be apparent to the parties involved.

An often-overlooked yet critical aspect of conflict resolution at home is follow-up. After reaching an agreement, periodically revisit the arrangement to ensure it still works for both parties. Relationships are dynamic, and what works today might need tweaking tomorrow. Checking in with each other ensures the agreement remains effective and shows ongoing commitment to mutual satisfaction.

Conflict resolution at home isn't a one-off event but an ongoing practice. It's a blend of empathy, effective communication, and strategic negotiation. By fostering these skills, we can transform conflicts into opportunities for deeper understanding and stronger bonds. So next time you face a disagreement at home, remember: you're not just resolving a conflict, you're building a more resilient and empathetic relationship, one conversation at a time.

Chapter 12: Mastering the Art of Closure

Negotiations are like orchestras, each player bringing their own instrument and intentions, yet the performance remains incomplete without a harmonious finale. This chapter illuminates the path to mastering the art of closure, often the linchpin determining not just the outcome but the perceived success of the entire negotiation. To reach a win-win agreement, both parties must feel heard, validated, and find their core interests met. Formalizing the deal transforms verbal promises into tangible commitments; it's where the handshake turns into ink on paper. Moreover, our work doesn't end with signatures. Post-negotiation strategies, including follow-ups and relationship maintenance, can turn a one-time beneficial agreement into long-term partnerships. By mastering closure, you're not just sealing a deal; you're opening doors to future opportunities and trust. This chapter will integrate the psychological finesse, strategic clarity, and empathetic communication that are critical for concluding negotiations effectively and inspiringly.

Reaching a Win-Win Agreement

Picture this: You're in a high-stakes negotiation that could make or break your business. You're not just fighting to hold onto your piece of the pie; you're working to make the pie itself bigger. That, at its core, is the essence of reaching a win-win agreement.

Imagine the negotiation table as a stage where both parties are co-stars in a collaborative performance. The goal isn't to leave the room with your counterpart feeling defeated. Instead, strive for a resolution where both parties walk away feeling like winners. This forms the foundation for lasting partnerships and ensures future collaborations will be just as fruitful, if not more so.

A win-win negotiation isn't about giving in or surrendering to the other party's demands. Rather, it's about understanding their needs, shedding light on your own priorities, and figuring out how the two can align. This approach helps to break down barriers and eliminate the zero-sum game mentality, fostering a spirit of cooperation rather than competition.

Getting to this point requires empathy. You've got to genuinely understand the interests, motivations, and even the anxieties of the other party. Empathy goes beyond saying, "I know how you feel." It's showing through your actions and words that you're trying to see the world through their eyes. When both parties feel heard and understood, the barriers of mistrust crumble, paving the way for a more amicable agreement.

However, there's a fine line between empathy and vulnerability. While understanding the other party's position is crucial, you mustn't compromise your own needs and values. Striking a balance is key. One way to maintain this balance is through effective communication. State your needs clearly and listen actively when the other party does the same.

Pragmatism also plays a crucial role. This means anchoring your discussions in reality, and being honest with yourself and the other party. Avoid grandstanding or creating unachievable expectations. Embrace a realistic outlook that focuses on achievable solutions. When both parties know what's on the table is fair and feasible, negotiations progress more smoothly.

Flexibility can't be overstated. Being rigid in your demands may project strength initially, but it can also stall negotiations. The art of closure requires a certain fluidity. Adaptability shows that you're not just interested in your own benefit but are also concerned about the deal's broader impact. This isn't weakness; it's strategic acumen.

So, let's talk specifics. Begin with an open dialogue that allows both sides to share their primary interests. Use this as a foundation to build options that cater to these interests. This isn't done in one fell swoop—it's iterative. As you uncover more about the other party's needs, reiterate and refine your offerings.

Take the case of integrative negotiations, specifically designed to expand the pie for all involved. Here, the focus shifts from what each party stands to lose or gain individually to what can be achieved collectively. It's about creating mutual value rather than fighting over existing value. This shift in perspective can lead to more innovative and beneficial solutions.

Consider hypothetical trading, where each party trades issues of lower priority but higher value to the other side. You may sacrifice something minor for you but critical for the other party, creating a win for them. They reciprocate similarly, achieving a balanced result. This strategy helps build a partnership mentality, which is invaluable for ongoing relationships.

Regularly check in to ensure all parties are on the same page. Mismatched expectations are often the root of unnecessary tension. Frequent validation ensures that both parties are aligned, preventing miscommunication and its resultant distrust. This doesn't mean micromanaging; it's more about periodic reconfirmation.

A conducive negotiation environment also holds great importance. This isn't just about the physical setting—although a comfortable setting does help—but the overall atmosphere. An environment free of hostility, built on mutual respect and open dialogue, clears the path for a win-win agreement. Establishing such an environment falls upon both parties, promoting shared responsibility in creating fruitful discussions.

Let's not ignore the role of timing. Each negotiation stage demands a different tempo. Pushing too hard too fast can backfire, but dragging on can exhaust both sides. Opt for a tempo that reflects the importance and complexity of the negotiations. Balance patience with a sense of urgency to keep the momentum steady without overwhelming the other party.

In the quest for a win-win outcome, you must remain vigilant of impasse signs. Sometimes, the other party might feel they're losing too much and retract. Rather than pushing back harder, consider reframing your proposals to highlight mutual benefits. Shifting the focus can reignite stalled negotiations and steer them back on track.

In collaboration, the power dynamics will inevitably shift. To ensure these shifts don't derail the negotiations, establish transparency from the get-go. Honesty about your intentions and non-negotiables creates a solid foundation, preventing unexpected surprises. This trust builds a negotiation where both sides strive toward mutual success.

Let's also delve into creative problem-solving, a cornerstone of win-win agreements. When stuck, think outside the box. Introduce unconventional solutions that meet core interests in novel ways. Creativity shows commitment beyond the surface, reinforcing that both parties are invested in reaching an agreement.

It's essential to also appreciate that win-win doesn't always mean equality. It means fairness and satisfaction based on each party's primary interests. Keep this in mind to avoid getting hung up on making everything evenly split. Sometimes, equity holds more value than equality.

Finally, rest on the principle of post-negotiation reflection. Once an agreement is reached, assess its components. Did it address everyone's core needs? Are both parties leaving the table satisfied and ready for future collaborations? Honest reflection helps fine-tune your negotiation skills, preparing you for even more successful win-win agreements down the road.

So as you step into your next negotiation, aim high, but be prepared to listen, adapt, and seek solutions that bring mutual benefit. Reaching a win-win agreement isn't just a tactic; it's a philosophy that, when practiced, carries over to every facet of your professional and personal life. It turns adversaries into allies and deals into partnerships, crafting a legacy of shared success.

Formalizing the Deal

So, you've navigated through all the obstacles, built rapport, employed your tactics, and now you're at the cusp of finalizing the negotiation. This is the moment where everything you've worked for comes together. But don't get complacent; this stage demands as much focus and precision as any other. Formalizing the deal is about transforming verbal agreements into binding commitments. And to do that effectively, you need to understand the elements that turn a handshake into a signature.

At this stage, details are not just important; they are everything. You need to make sure that every aspect of what's been agreed upon is clearly documented. Misunderstandings now can lead to disputes later. So, ensure that your contract or agreement is comprehensive and leaves no room for ambiguity. Focus on clarity and specificity. Operating under the assumption that "it's understood" without putting it in writing is a recipe for disaster.

One critical step in formalizing a deal is to revisit the objectives that both parties outlined at the beginning. Are all the key points addressed? Are the deliverables, timelines, and payment terms clearly defined? By cross-referencing the final agreement with your original goals, you can catch any discrepancies that may have been overlooked in the heat of negotiation. This is your chance to ensure that the agreement fulfills your needs and expectations fully.

It's equally vital to involve legal expertise at this point. A lawyer can help you draft a contract that is enforceable and fair. They can spot potential pitfalls and suggest necessary clauses that protect your interests. This step not only helps in mitigating risk but also adds a layer of professionalism to the entire process. No matter how minor the deal may seem, always err on the side of caution by getting legal advice.

Reviewing the terms with the other party is also essential. Bring them back to the table to go over the written agreement. This isn't just about ensuring they understand the terms; it's also an opportunity to confirm that everyone is on the same page. This mutual review can eliminate future grievances and build an additional layer of trust. Sometimes, even well-intentioned partners can interpret verbal agreements differently.

Effective communication continues to be your most valuable tool here. As you discuss the terms, explain the reasons behind each clause. Transparency can prevent misunderstandings and illuminate any areas that may need further negotiation. This conversation isn't just about dotting i's and crossing t's; it's another opportunity for collaboration.

Once the terms are clear and both parties are in agreement, the next step is the formal signing. Make sure that all relevant stakeholders are present to sign the documents. Digital signatures have become more acceptable, especially in remote or online negotiations, but ensure that these are legally binding in your jurisdiction. You can't afford to cut corners here.

Recording the deal is a critical step that's often overlooked. Keep all the original documents in a secure place, both digitally and physically. This isn't just a formality; it's a safeguard for future reference. You'll want to have immediate access to these documents should any questions or disputes arise. Proper record-keeping can save you a lot of trouble down the line.

After the ink has dried, it's essential to remind yourself that this isn't the end. Post-negotiation strategies come into play immediately after the deal is sealed. Follow up with a summary email reiterating the main points of the agreement, the responsibilities of each party, and the next steps. This step not only reinforces the commitments made but also ensures that there is a mutual understanding moving forward.

Continuous communication remains key. Regular check-ins can help maintain the relationship and ensure the deal is being implemented as agreed. You've put in the hard work to reach this point; don't let poor follow-up undermine your success. Foster the relationship as you move forward, ensuring all parties are satisfied and any issues are promptly addressed.

The art of formalizing the deal is as much about closure as it is about opening new avenues. A thoroughly documented and clearly understood agreement can pave the way for future opportunities. When both parties feel secure about the commitments made, this can lead to long-term partnerships. You've moved from negotiation to a solid foundation for continual collaboration.

Trust, once again, is a recurring theme. Formalizing the deal with transparency and care builds trust. You not only demonstrate your commitment to the agreement but also your commitment to the other party. This trust can be invaluable as you move forward, providing a reliable base for future negotiations.

In summary, to master the art of formalizing a deal: emphasize clarity in documentation, involve legal expertise, ensure mutual understanding through review, safeguard your records, and follow through with vigilant post-negotiation strategies. Each step reinforces the work you've done and sets the stage for future success.

As you proceed into the future, remember that formalizing the deal is not a mere checkpoint but a critical phase that shapes the outcome of your negotiations. This is where the real value is realized, where agreements turn into tangible results. Keep honing this skill, for in mastering this art, you're ensuring that your hard-earned victories leave a lasting, positive impact.

Post-Negotiation Strategies

You've navigated through the stormy seas of negotiation, and the deal is inked. But, contrary to popular belief, the negotiation process doesn't truly end when agreements are signed. Handling the post-negotiation landscape with finesse is imperative to ensure long-term success and sustain the relationships built during the process. This chapter will illuminate the strategies that can help you solidify the gains, foster lasting partnerships, and minimize any potential backlash.

First and foremost, maintaining communication is crucial. The ink might have dried, but that doesn't mean the conversation stops. A common pitfall is "deal and disappear," where participants go silent after an agreement. Avoid this. Use follow-up emails, phone calls, or even face-to-face meetings to continue nurturing the relationship. Doing this not only reaffirms your commitment but also provides a platform for addressing any unresolved issues.

Next, it's important to evaluate the outcomes. Did the results align with your initial objectives? Conducting a thorough post-mortem analysis can provide insights into what worked and what didn't. This is not just about self-reflection but includes reaching out to the other party for their feedback. Their perspective can offer a fresh angle you may have missed and help identify areas for improvement in future negotiations.

The establishment of a feedback loop is another powerful tool. Creating a mechanism where both parties can share ongoing feedback helps to keep expectations aligned. It can be a structured process through scheduled meetings or a more informal approach via regular communication channels.

The key is to make sure it's a two-way street, fostering a culture of mutual respect and continual improvement.

After the agreement is in place, documenting everything meticulously is vital. Never underestimate the power of having a detailed record. This documentation should go beyond the main contractual terms to include any verbal understandings or handshake agreements. Recording these nuances ensures everyone is on the same page and can prevent potential disputes down the line.

Strategic alignment is another crucial aspect. Both parties often have broader organizational goals that the immediate agreement serves. Regular check-ins to discuss how the deal's implementation aligns with these larger objectives can foster cooperation and make adjustments easier if needed. This alignment ensures that the relationship is more than transactional; it becomes transformational.

Consider setting up joint teams or committees to oversee the implementation of the agreement. These collaborative groups can tackle any emerging issues promptly and work towards continuous improvement. By embedding a structure for ongoing dialogue, you bolster the relationship's strength and adaptability.

Acknowledging and celebrating milestones can also be beneficial. Whether it's achieving a significant project phase or hitting a performance target, recognition reinforces positive behavior and energizes the partnership. It doesn't have to be extravagant—a simple acknowledgement can go a long way in building goodwill and motivation.

One often overlooked area is addressing buyer's remorse. It's not uncommon for one party to feel some level of regret or second-guessing after sealing a deal. Proactively addressing these concerns can mitigate dissatisfaction. Engage with the other party, reassure them of the agreement's mutual benefits, and demonstrate your commitment to making things work.

Active dispute resolution mechanisms should also be in place. The reality of post-negotiation is that issues will arise. Having a predefined process to manage disagreements can save time, reduce tensions, and preserve the relationship. Whether it's through mediation, arbitration, or a mutually agreed-upon process, clarity on dispute resolution procedures is vital.

Trust is a dynamic quality that must be continually earned and validated. Transparency is foundational here. If unforeseen challenges or delays occur, being upfront about them builds credibility. Conversely, concealing issues erodes trust and can unravel all the efforts invested in the negotiation process.

Leveraging data and analytics can be another post-negotiation strategy. Having measurable benchmarks enables both parties to track progress and assess performance objectively. Analytics can provide early warnings for potential issues, allowing for proactive adjustments instead of reactive firefighting.

Creating win-win scenarios doesn't stop at the negotiation table. Post-negotiation is an ongoing process of reaffirming and finding new intersections of mutual benefit. Regularly revisit the agreement to uncover new opportunities for collaboration or mutual gain. This adaptability fosters a more resilient and innovative partnership.

Lastly, consider conducting a formal debrief with your team. Internal debriefings help capture lessons learned and institutionalize them for future negotiations. Reflect on aspects such as preparation, communication, and execution. Document these findings and share them within your organization to elevate your collective negotiating know-how.

Effective post-negotiation strategies transform a mere deal into a sustainable, long-term partnership. By committing to ongoing communication, rigorous evaluation, and adaptive alignment, you pave the way for lasting success. The art of closure is not about shutting the door but opening it to continuous improvement and mutual growth.

Conclusion

As we reach the final pages of this journey into the art and science of negotiation, it's clear that negotiation isn't just a skill—it's a mindset. Throughout these chapters, we've explored fundamental techniques, delved into the psychology behind decision-making, and uncovered the intricate dance of building rapport and trust. Each strategy and tactic you've encountered is a stepping stone toward becoming a master negotiator.

Mastery in negotiation, as in any field, requires practice and a willingness to continuously learn. It's not about memorizing formulas but about understanding principles deeply enough to apply them fluidly in all situations. This flexibility allows you to adapt to the unexpected, turning potential stumbling blocks into opportunities for growth and success. The real-world examples and case studies we've examined demonstrate that even the most seasoned negotiators encounter challenges—but with resilience and a strategic approach, they turn these challenges into triumphs.

The heart of successful negotiation lies in preparation. Meticulous research and thoughtful analysis pave the way for effective strategies. Knowing your objectives and priorities, as well as understanding the other party's interests, transforms the negotiation from a mere transactional interaction into a purposeful dialogue. When you're prepared, you're not swayed by surprises; instead, you're positioned to steer the conversation toward mutual benefit.

Consider the importance of empathy and communication. As we've discussed, building trust isn't just about presenting your case—it's about genuinely connecting with the other party. Active listening, mindful body language, and the power of empathy turn adversaries into allies. In those moments, negotiation transcends the exchange of terms; it becomes a human endeavor based on respect and understanding.

Effective negotiators understand the balance between competition and collaboration. The strategic deployment of both competitive and collaborative approaches, depending on the context, ensures a more nuanced and successful negotiation outcome. Recognizing when to push for your interests and when to seek common ground is a hallmark of a master negotiator. Our discussions about BATNA (Best Alternative to a Negotiated Agreement) and ZOPA (Zone of Possible Agreement) have underscored the importance of strategic flexibility and awareness.

Overcoming obstacles is an inevitable part of negotiation. Whether dealing with difficult personalities, managing conflicts, or breaking deadlocks, the ability to remain calm and composed is invaluable. The techniques for overcoming these challenges, discussed in depth, have shown that preparation and patience often triumph over aggression and haste. These skills are not only valuable in the negotiating room but extend to various aspects of personal and professional life.

Understanding cultural differences and leveraging technology effectively can also broaden your horizons. As the world becomes more interconnected, the ability to navigate cross-cultural negotiations and utilize online tools enhances your negotiation repertoire. Being sensitive to cultural nuances and ethical considerations ensures not only success but also a legacy of respect and integrity.

Ethics form the backbone of any successful negotiation. Establishing clear ethical boundaries and understanding the consequences of unethical behavior are crucial for long-term success. The case studies on ethical dilemmas have illustrated how integrity can sustain relationships and build a reputation that far outweighs any temporary gain achieved through unscrupulous means.

Finally, applying these principles to personal life reinforces the universal applicability of negotiation skills. Whether negotiating within your family, for personal gains, or resolving conflicts at home, these skills enrich relationships and foster a collaborative environment. The techniques you've learned in a professional context seamlessly translate into personal interactions, enhancing every facet of your daily life.

Epilogue

Looking Forward

As you close this book, remember that negotiation is an evolving field. The landscape of negotiation will continue to change with advancements in technology, shifts in global markets, and emerging cultural dynamics. Staying informed and adaptable will always give you an edge.

Take what you've learned here and apply it. Practice makes perfect, but so does reflection. After each negotiation, evaluate what worked and what didn't. Learn from every experience and continuously hone your skills.

Empowerment Through Knowledge

The knowledge you now possess is your toolkit. Whether you're negotiating a business deal, mediating a team conflict, or simply trying to get the best price on a purchase, you are equipped to approach each situation with confidence and clarity.

Empowerment comes from knowing not only the theory but the practical application of these principles. You have the power to influence outcomes, build stronger relationships, and achieve your goals. By implementing these strategies, you'll find that you not only become a better negotiator but also a more effective leader, communicator, and decision-maker.

Reflect on the stories, studies, and strategies we've discussed. They're more than just examples—they are frameworks for you to build upon. Consider them as a foundation upon which you can innovate and personalize your approach. The ultimate goal is to find your unique negotiating style, one that aligns with your values and goals.

The Journey Continues

Negotiation, much like life, is a continuous journey rather than a destination. As you move forward, remember that every negotiation is an opportunity to learn and grow. Take each experience, whether successful or challenging, as a lesson to refine your skills.

Stay curious. Keep exploring the ever-evolving landscape of negotiation. The principles you've learned here are timeless, but the context in which you apply them will always be dynamic. Embrace this dynamism and allow it to fuel your growth.

A Call to Action

Finally, take action. The knowledge you've gained is powerful, but only if you put it into practice. Approach your next negotiation with confidence, armed with the tools and insights you've gathered. Whether in the boardroom or at the dinner table, approach each interaction with the intent to understand, collaborate, and succeed.

Remember, you're not just aiming for short-term wins but building a legacy of effective negotiation. Your influence extends beyond individual deals, contributing to sustainable relationships and long-term success.

This is your journey to mastery. So, go forth and negotiate with wisdom, empathy, and confidence. The world awaits your expertise.

Appendix A: Appendix

In this appendix, we aim to provide you with additional resources, tools, and insights that complement the concepts discussed throughout this book. Whether you're an experienced negotiator or just beginning your journey, these materials can serve as invaluable aids in your continuous development. Let's dive in.

Resources for Further Reading

Continuous learning is vital for becoming a master negotiator. The following books and articles are recommended for deepening your understanding and sharpening your skills:

- **"Getting to Yes: Negotiating Agreement Without Giving In" by Roger Fisher and William Ury** – A classic in negotiation literature, this book offers practical advice on how to negotiate without compromising your core principles.
- **"Influence: The Psychology of Persuasion" by Robert B. Cialdini** – This book delves into the science of why people say "yes" and how to apply these insights to negotiation scenarios.
- "Difficult Conversations: How to Discuss What Matters Most" by Douglas Stone, Bruce Patton, and Sheila Heen – **A guide to navigating tough talks with confidence and clarity.**
- **"Never Split the Difference: Negotiating As If Your Life Depended On It" by Chris Voss** – Written by a former FBI hostage negotiator, this book offers high-stakes negotiation strategies that can be applied to business and personal life.

- **Articles from the Harvard Negotiation Law Review** – A wealth of peer-reviewed articles that cover various aspects of negotiation theory and practice. Check out their website for more information.

Acknowledgments

Completing this book would have been impossible without the support and insight of numerous individuals. A heartfelt thank you goes out to:

- Our Expert Contributors: Your diverse experiences and rich knowledge made this book a treasure trove of practical wisdom. Special thanks to industry veterans, academics, and seasoned negotiators who contributed valuable case studies and anecdotes.
- The Editorial Team: Your relentless commitment to excellence helped transform initial drafts into polished chapters. Your attention to detail and rigorous standards ensured that every page adds value to the reader.
- Family and Friends: Your unwavering encouragement and patience provided the emotional support needed to bring this project to fruition. Thank you for believing in the importance of this work.

Personal growth in negotiation is a lifelong endeavor. The resources and acknowledgments mentioned here are just the beginning. Stay curious, stay dedicated, and you will undoubtedly reach new heights in your negotiation skills. Good luck, and happy negotiating!